China Past—
China Future

中國古往今來

ALDEN R. CARTER

FRANKLIN WATTS

NEW YORK · CHICAGO · LONDON · TORONTO · SYDNEY

Map by Gary S. Tong

Chinese calligraphy by
Harry Kwong Hang Soong

Photographs copyright © Reuters/Bettmann Newsphotos: frontis,
pp. 27,28, 29, 30, 31, 32; The Freer Gallery of Art, The Smithsonian
Institution, Washington, D.C.: p. 1; New York Public Library,
Picture Collection: pp. 2, 4 top, 9,10, 11, 12, 13, 14, 15, 16, 28, 19 top
and bottom left, 20 bottom, 21 top; The Nelson-Atkins Museum of
Art, Kansas City, Mo., (gift of Gronson Trevor in honor of his father, John Trevor), 76-10/12: p. 3; the Bettmann Archive: pp. 5, 14,
17 bottom, 21 bottom, 26 top; North Wind Picture Archives: pp.
6,7 bottom, 17 top; Photo Researchers, Inc./Omikron: p. 8; Histori-
cal Pictures/Stock Montage: pp. 15, 19 bottom right;
UPI/Bettmann Newsphotos: pp. 20 top, 22, 23 bottom, 24, 25; the
Hutchison Library: p. 23 top; Wide World Photos: p. 26 bottom.

Library of Congress Cataloging-in-Publication Data

Carter, Alden R.
China past-China future / Alden R. Carter.
p. cm.
Includes bibliographical references and index.
Summary: A history of China with an overview of life today and a
look at its possible future, considering an increasingly young
population which is dissatisfied with communism.
ISBN 0-531-11161-X
1. China—History—Juvenile literature. [1. China—History]
I. Title.
DS736.C226   1994
951—dc20   93-13537 CIP AC

Contents

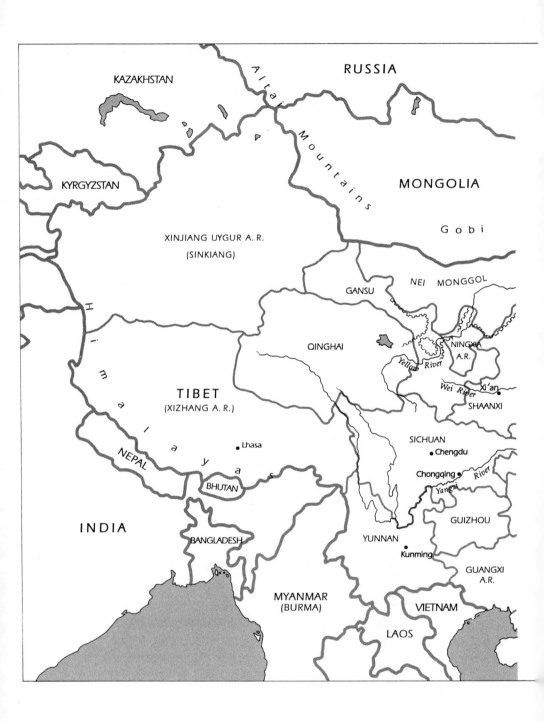

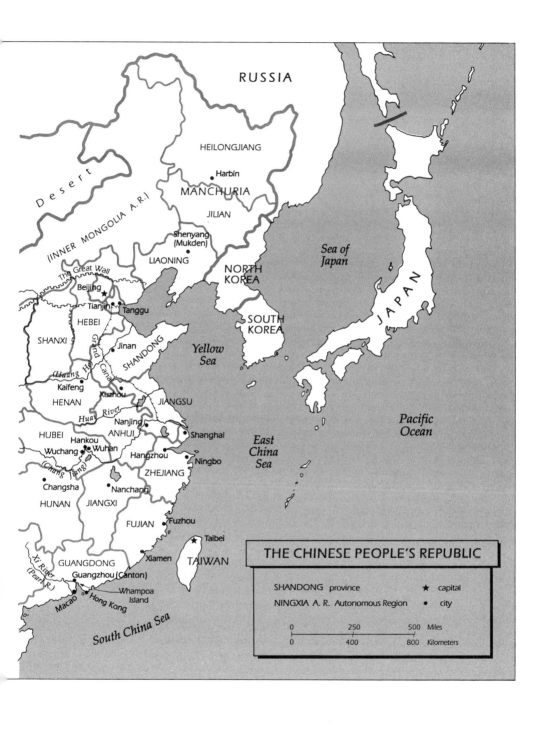

RUSSIA

HEILONGJIANG

• Harbin

MANCHURIA

JILIAN

(INNER MONGOLIA A.R.)

Desert

Shenyang
(Mukden)

LIAONING

The Great Wall

Beijing ★

Tianjin • • Tanggu

HEBEI

SHANXI

Grand Canal

• Jinan

SHANDONG

(Huang He)

Kaifeng •

Xuzhou •

HENAN

Huai River

Nanjing •

HUBEI

ANHUI

Hankou

Wuchang • • Wuhan

(Chang Jiang)

Hangzhou •

Changsha •

• Nanchang

ZHEJIANG

HUNAN

JIANGXI

FUJIAN

• Fuzhou

★ Taibei

Xiamen •

TAIWAN

Xi River
(Pearl R.)

GUANGDONG

Guangzhou (Canton) •

Whampoa
Island

Macao

Hong Kong

NORTH
KOREA

SOUTH
KOREA

Yellow
Sea

Sea of
Japan

JAPAN

Pacific
Ocean

East
China
Sea

Shanghai •

• Ningbo

South China Sea

THE CHINESE PEOPLE'S REPUBLIC

SHANDONG province   ★ capital

NINGXIA A. R. Autonomous Region   • city

| 0 | 250 | 500 | Miles |
| 0 | 400 | 800 | Kilometers |

Dedication

For Dr. David Wen-Wei Chang and all the scholars who have devoted their lives to a better understanding between China and the West.

Acknowledgments

Many thanks to all who helped with *China Past–China Future*, particularly my editor, Lorna Greenberg; my mother, Hilda Carter Fletcher; my friends Dean Markwardt and Alice Chang; my wife, Carol; and our China-traveling companions Don and Georgette Beyer. I owe special thanks to Dr. David Wen-Wei Chang, who, in both physical and figurative terms, guided me through the wonders of China. Without his expertise, wisdom, and endless patience, this book could not have been written.

The Spelling and Pronunciation of Chinese Words

Unlike English words, Chinese words are not spelled with letters representing spoken sounds. Instead, each word is written as an ideogram (or character) representing an idea. By combining various characters, the writer can express different ideas. For example, the character 説 "speak" and the character 明 "bright" together mean "explanation:" 説明.

Chinese has at least 50,000 ideograms, and probably no one knows them all. About 6,000 characters are commonly used, and the government has simplified about 3,000 to ease the task of learning written Chinese. Literacy is particularly valuable in China because the pronunciation of Chinese varies widely from region to region, while the written language is universal. All schools in China now teach Mandarin, the most widely spoken dialect, as part of an effort to standardize pronunciation across China.

A number of systems have been devised to spell Chinese words in the Latin alphabet used in most of the West. Chinese words in this book are spelled according to the pinyin system adopted by the State Council of the People's Republic of China in 1979 to replace the Wade-Giles system developed in Great Britain in the nineteenth century. Since Chinese is a tonal language, no system can exactly duplicate the actual spoken sounds of Chinese words. Nevertheless, a fair approximation can be made by using the equivalent English sounds for pinyin consonants, with these exceptions:

> c is pronounced *ts* when it is the initial sound in a word
> q is pronounced *ch*
> x is pronounced as a soft *sh*, nearly *sy*
> z is pronounced *dz*
> zh is pronounced *j*

Chinese vowels are most commonly pronounced:

> a as in the *ah* in f*a*r
> e as in the *eh* in b*e*t
> i as in the *ee* in fr*ee*, except when it is a final vowel following *c*, *s*, or *z*, when it is pronounced *uh*, or following *ch*, *sh*, or *zh* when it is pronounced *ur*
> o as in the *aw* in l*a*w
> u as in the *oo* in p*oo*l

When two vowels are written together, each retains an individual sound. Hence, *Mao* is pronounced like *mou* in *mou*th.

The Chinese characters that appear along with the chapter numbers are pronounced as follows:

one	一	yee	six	六	liu
two	二	er	seven	七	chee
three	三	san	eight	八	ba
four	四	sse	nine	九	jiu
five	五	woo	ten	十	shi

Foreword

BY DAVID WEN-WEI CHANG, PH.D.

Since Marco Polo dictated his famous *Travels* seven hundred years ago, Western readers have come to know China through thousands of books and countless articles. Yet China remains an enigma to most Westerners. It is vital to the future of an increasingly interconnected world for writers, scholars, and all people of goodwill to continue their efforts to correct the misconceptions, untruths, and prejudices that have so long plagued the relationship between China and the West. It is my hope that Alden R. Carter's splendid new book on China will introduce great numbers of American young people to China's history, present reality, and hopes for the future—a future in which America and the rest of the world will have an increasingly significant interest.

It is difficult for Americans, accustomed as they are to a rapidly changing society where the past often seems irrelevant, to appreciate the incredible length of China's unique history and the durability of so many of its political and cultural institutions. Until this century, China's governmental, social, and economic framework had changed little in over 2,000 years, despite devastating invasions, frequent internal rebellions, and a multitude of natural disasters. With the exception of India, no other major nation has known such an enduring continuity from the ancient past to the threshold of the modern era.

In this century, China has been convulsed by two great revolutions. Dr. Sun Yat-sen's Nationalist Revolution of 1911 held out the promise of Western-style democracy in China. But Japanese aggression, Western indifference, and China's own unreadiness combined to doom Dr. Sun's vision. The Communist Revolution of 1949 succeeded in unifying the nation and ridding China of foreign interference in its internal affairs. But Mao Zedong's radical social and economic agenda became a monumental disaster. Only the counterbalance of Premier Zhou Enlai and his fellow pragmatists prevented the Chinese state from capsizing during the stormy era that ended with the death of Mao in 1976.

Like the lives of hundreds of millions of other Chinese who were the victims of excessive revolution, my life has reflected many of the wrenching changes in my homeland. My second oldest brother was killed in 1948 during the civil war between the Nationalists and the Communists. In 1949, I left China—not entirely of my own free will—in the Nationalist evacuation to Taiwan. Four years later, I came to the United States as a student, with the full intention of soon returning to China. While I studied and taught in the United States and my eldest brother served as a general in the Nationalist army on Taiwan, my third brother worked as a farmer in the People's Republic of China (PRC). For him, life was most difficult as he suffered years of humiliation at the hands of the Communist authorities for his relationship to us and because he had owned a few more acres than the average farmer before the revolution.

Communication with families in the PRC was so difficult in the quarter century following the Communist Revolution that I did not even learn of my mother's death in 1955 until nearly twenty years later. Through the 1960s and 1970s, I wrote and taught about China, hoping that my experience in two cultures would help bridge the gulf between them. In 1968, I became a United States citizen. Finally, in 1979, with relations improving between the United States and the PRC, I was at last able to return to China to visit my mother's grave and to see again the relatives I had left behind.

I offer my story only as a mild example of what millions of Chinese suffered in an upheaval the like of which few in the West can imagine. Since China again opened its doors, I have returned a half dozen times to study firsthand the immense changes communism has brought to China, and to share with the citizens of my homeland something of what I have learned in four decades of living in the West. It has been my privilege to lecture to large numbers of students and intellectuals, and to meet on frequent occasions with scholars and government leaders for whom the United States often seems as impenetrable an enigma as China seems to American intellectuals.

It has also been my privilege to guide university groups of professors, public school teachers, and other interested Americans on their first visit to China. On one of these trips, I was joined by the novelist and nonfiction writer Alden Carter and his photographer–social worker wife, Carol, who were gathering material for a book on China. Carol's job was difficult because many Chinese dislike having their picture taken by strangers, and the incredible diversity of China is exceedingly difficult to capture on film. Yet Carol, with her disarming smile and her sharp eye for the best image and angle, managed to capture both the people and the physical reality of China.

While Carol snapped roll after roll of film, Al asked a flood of questions. His insatiable curiosity, his demand for exhaustive and rigorously accurate answers, and his intuitive ability to enter into the spirit of what it means to be Chinese made *Modern China* (Franklin Watts, 1986) a joy to read and—with Carol's photographs—an invaluable source for young people.

During the preparation of Al's second book on China, *China Past–China Future*, it has again been my great pleasure to read and comment on preliminary drafts of the manuscript. I know of no other book that provides such a concise yet accurate introduction for readers of all ages to the political, cultural, and social institutions that make China a nation of such profound fascination. In vivid yet simple language, the author provides the reader with a remarkably comprehensive picture of the tremendous sweep of Chinese history from the ancient past to the troubled present, concluding with a clear and insightful look into the probable shape of China's future.

The Chinese people have known terrible disappointment with the failure of two revolutionary systems in this century. Since the late 1970s, the pragmatic Communist leaders led by Deng Xiaoping have steered China onto a new course of economic development. Yet their insistence on pursuing rapid economic change without a correspondingly rapid expansion of political and human rights has created a volatile mixture of rising expectations and unsatisfied hopes. The people's demands for openness, fairness, and justice gave rise to the massive Tiananmen Square demonstrations so brutally suppressed in the spring of 1989. But the government crackdown did not destroy the people's hopes for democracy and human rights—hopes that will eventually find realization in the creation of a new order in China.

I share Alden Carter's optimism about the future development of democracy and economic opportunity in China. The process may be long, because the obstacles are immense. But the resiliency, courage, and adaptability of the Chinese people remain undiminished as the world approaches the end of a tumultuous century. China is a land of both continuity and change, where tradition and modernity exist side by side. In their quest for modernization, the 800 million people of rural China will not readily accept the Western example of urbanization and disregard for the past. Instead, they will use their rural-based and family-oriented traditions to develop a humane social democracy unlike anything the world has ever known—a system that by its example alone will have momentous influence far beyond China's borders.

It is my hope—as it is Carter's—that the opening decades of the twenty-first century will celebrate the dawn of a new era in the history of East and West; that the generation now growing to adulthood will reach out across the barriers that separated all previous generations to build a world of peace, fairness, and mutual understanding. As a small but significant step in that process, I invite young readers, their parents, and their teachers to turn now to Alden Carter's stirring account of China's history of glory and suffering, of its challenging present and extraordinary potential for the future, and of the eternal courage and dignity of the Chinese people.

DAVID WEN-WEI CHANG

Introduction: Facing the Tanks

The column of tanks clanked down the wide avenue running west from Tiananmen Square at the heart of China's capital of Beijing. A slender young man in black trousers and a white shirt hurried to the center of Changan Boulevard to stand unmoving in the path of the 36-ton metal monsters. High atop a nearby building, a photographer began recording a scene that would become famous around the world.

China was in turmoil in this spring of 1989. For a month, Chinese students had occupied Tiananmen Square, demanding democratic reforms in the Communist system that had governed China for forty years. All over China, students, workers, farmers, and people of every walk of life demonstrated in support of the democracy movement launched by the Beijing students. People in the working-class neighborhoods south and west of Tiananmen Square took on the special role of protecting the students against the tanks and soldiers gathering on the outskirts of the city.

The protests threatened the aging leaders in control of the People's Republic of China. In the early morning hours of June 4, 1989, they sent the army to smash the democracy movement. Thousands of soldiers—many of them unwilling—and scores of tanks and armored personnel carriers blasted their way through the working-class neighborhoods. Along Changan Boulevard, hundreds of people were shot or crushed to death as the armored vehicles crashed through barricades. The soldiers routed the students in Tiananmen Square and then set about stamping out the riots convulsing whole sections of this city of ten million.

The young man in the white shirt had no doubt seen the mangled dead and the bicycles crushed to the thickness of cardboard, but he stood his ground as the tanks approached. With an abrupt change in the growl of its engine, the lead tank clanked to a halt, its comrades jerking to a stop all the way up the long line stretching back to the square. The hidden driver shouted for the young man to move, but he only made an angry gesture with the coat draped over his right arm. The tank started again, swinging right as it tried to pull around him. The young man dashed to his left, again planting himself in front of the tank. The tank swerved to the right, but again the young man ran to put his body in its path. The tank edged forward. The young man straightened to attention and stood immobile. The tank stopped.

For a long moment, neither tank nor man moved. Then the young man clambered up its front to pound on the hatch and demand an explanation for the violence inflicted by the People's Liberation Army on the people of China. The hatch opened and a young soldier popped his head out. What the two said to each other we do not know. Perhaps the soldier angrily defended his obedience to orders. Or perhaps he wept at the memory of what he and his comrades had done. Moments later, onlookers—probably friends concerned for the young man's safety—hurried to the tank, pulled him down, and rushed him away. The soldier disappeared inside the tank. Its engine revved and, with the other tanks following through a haze of diesel smoke, the column ground its way down the boulevard whose name translates as "the Avenue of Eternal Peace."

Smuggled out of China to be broadcast and printed countless times, the pictures of the lone young man facing down the tanks touched people all over the world. Here were images that dispelled the confusion most people felt in trying to understand the complexity of political events in China. A simple truth shone through: In the spring of 1989, the Chinese people had stood in the path of the tanks, challenging with their bodies and their spirits all the might, steel, and violence of a tyrannical government. They had been defeated, but they would try again—attempting with raw courage and deep belief to seize control of their lives and the future of the most populous nation on earth.

1 China: Most Populous Nation on Earth

The People's Republic of China (PRC) is one of the world's largest nations, slightly greater in area than the United States. (Only Russia and Canada are bigger.) Including the island of Taiwan, which has had a separate government since 1949, China has an area of 3,696,100 square miles (9,572,900 sq. km). Almost every kind of geography can be found in China: steppes, deserts, mountains, tropical lowlands, pine forests, and flood-washed river valleys. In all, about two-thirds of China is either mountainous or desert.

Many types of climate reflect China's geographical diversity. The south is very wet and hot much of the year. North of the Yangzi River, summers are milder and winters are dry and cold. In Tibet and Mongolia, temperatures plunge far below zero in winter. In the great western deserts, there are areas where it will not rain for years and summer temperatures climb over 100 degrees Fahrenheit (38° C).

Eastern China has some of the most heavily populated areas on earth. Fully 90 percent of China's 1.15 billion people live on only 15 percent of the land. Half of China is sparsely settled, with only 4 percent of the population. The PRC is divided into twenty-two provinces, three self-governing municipalities (the capital Beijing and the huge cities of Tianjin and Shanghai), and five autonomous regions. The autonomous regions supposedly have independent governments functioning under the guidance of the central government, but there is little real independence. Tibet, for many centuries an independent nation, is particularly restless under the heavy hand of the Beijing government.

RIVERS OF SORROW AND LIFE

China's great rivers have played a major part in Chinese history. The most famous is the Yangzi (also called the Chang Jiang), which divides southern from central China. Some 3,950 miles (6,360 km) long, the Yangzi is the third longest river in the world after the Nile and the Amazon. The Yangzi is a great thoroughfare for ships and boats carrying goods and passengers through an area that is home for some 300 million people. Near the coast the river is 30 miles (48 km) wide and deep enough for oceangoing tankers and freighters steaming upriver to China's largest city, the port of Shanghai.

Another mighty river divides central from northern China. The Yellow River, or Huang Ho, was known for generations as "the river of sorrows." It has flooded 1,500 times in recorded history, killing hundreds of thousands and driving millions from their homes. Yet the river is a blessing to the people, too. Every year its waters carry millions of tons of silt down from the highlands. The silt turns the water a deep yellow, giving the river its name. The river deposits the silt as a layer of rich soil on the floodplain, producing fertile farmland.

China's many rivers empty into the Pacific Ocean. China has a 4,000-mile (6,440-km) coastline, and the Chinese have long used the coastal waters for fishing and trading.

TRANSPORTATION

China's 68,000 miles (110,000 km) of inland waterways include an incredible system of canals built over more than 2,000 years. According to a conservative government estimate, 944 million tons (858 million metric tons) of freight and 458 million passengers traveled on the system in 1988.

The PRC's road system is primitive by Western standards. Most of the roads are narrow and unpaved, and there are no true superhighways. In total, China has less than 15 percent of the road mileage of the United States and only 2.2 percent of the vehicles. Since few Chinese can afford to own cars or trucks, bicycles are more than a casual means of travel. Morning and evening, city streets are crowded with workers cycling to or from work. In the countryside, peasants pile seemingly impossible loads on bicycles before pedaling to market.

China's railroads are among the most heavily used in the world, carrying 170 times as many passengers as do railroads in the United States. In contrast, China's domestic airline system is small and much of its equipment is outdated. In 1988, air travel in China amounted to less than 3.5 percent of the passenger miles recorded by airlines in the United States.

NATURAL RESOURCES

China has a shortage of good farmland. Only about 16 percent of the country is well suited to farming. Land that would be rejected as completely unsuitable in many countries is farmed with great care and skill by China's farmers, generally known as peasants. In many areas, they have sculpted entire mountains into step-like terraces to gain more farmland. The hard work of the peasants has made China one of the world's leaders in the production of rice, wheat, soybeans, tobacco, tea, and cotton.

China has vast natural resources for energy and industry, ranking among the world's leaders in coal, iron ore, uranium, tungsten, and tin production. A major effort is under way to develop vast offshore oil fields and to harness the hydroelectric potential of China's rivers.

THE PEOPLE OF CHINA

The population of China is huge. More than 1.15 billion people—roughly one out of every five people on earth—live in the PRC. Three-quarters of the people reside in rural areas, the vast majority working as farmers. (In the United States fewer than three people in a hundred are farmers.)

Over 90 percent of the Chinese are members of the Han race, named after an ancient royal family so respected by its subjects that they began calling themselves the "children of Han." Most Han Chinese are shorter and slighter than the average person in Western nations such as the United States, but there are also many tall and big-boned Chinese. Although almost all Han Chinese have brown eyes and straight black hair, skin coloring and facial features vary widely.

In addition to the Han majority, some fifty-five minorities live in the PRC. Some minorities number only a few thousand, while others have millions of members. Most of the minorities make their homes in the vast, sparsely populated western and northwestern regions of China. The hardy Tibetans live "on the roof of the world"—a high plateau north of the Himalayas. Much farther north, China's Mongols live in a land of wide prairies called steppes. The Dai people live in tropical

Yunnan, bordering Vietnam. Many of the Hakka minority live on colorful fishing boats on the southern coast and rarely go ashore. Some of the minorities were originally independent peoples, whose homelands were absorbed by the Chinese empire. Others were immigrants from distant lands, who came originally to conquer or to trade. Still others are racially Han Chinese but long ago adopted religions and accompanying lifestyles far different from the Han majority.

POPULATION CONTROL

With population growth threatening to outstrip China's resources, the government is waging a vigorous campaign to control the birthrate. Posters, newspapers, and radio and television announcements preach the government's one-child-per-family policy and promote the use of birth control. By law, the minimum age for marriage is twenty-two for men and twenty for women, but marriage before the mid-twenties is discouraged. A first child receives educational, housing, and medical benefits from the government, but a couple has to assume these costs for a second child. If a woman becomes pregnant a third time, the government pressures the couple to abort the pregnancy. Those who insist on having the child risk heavy fines and the loss of privileges.

The government's population planners battle deeply rooted Chinese traditions. For centuries, rural Chinese considered large families a blessing. With few laborsaving machines, many hands were needed to raise a crop. Famine, disease, and war cost the lives of many children long before they reached adulthood, so a large family was necessary to guarantee security for the parents in their old age.

Since the responsibility of caring for aged parents fell to the eldest surviving son, male children were much preferred. As in many other cultures, unwanted female infants and sickly male infants were sometimes drowned or left exposed to the elements to die. Marriages were arranged by parents, and a young couple often entered into marriage as total strangers. Once the bride entered her in-laws' home, she would remain subservient to her mother-in-law for years, in many cases not leaving the family compound for the rest of her life.

Although arranged marriages and many of the other confining traditions are now outlawed, the preference for boys remains strong. The government has put great effort into convincing Chinese parents of the equal worth of girls, but the persistence of "the boy preference" has made it necessary to add flexibility to the one-child-per-family rule. Parents in rural areas can now have a second child without penalty if their first was a girl or was born physically handicapped. National minorities are largely exempt from birth-control rules.

Chinese family traditions are very strong, and Chinese adults are doting parents and grandparents. Since most young people work, a child is often left in the care of a grandparent living in the home. If this arrangement is not possible, the child is usually placed in a government child-care facility. Because of the long Chinese workweek, some children see their parents only on weekends.

EDUCATION

Before the Communist government came to power in 1949, some 80 percent of the people were illiterate. The government has pushed a massive program of adult and child education into the far corners of the country. Today, about 80 percent of the population is literate. However, with a population so huge, China still has over 200 million people unable to read or write.

Kindergartens accept children as young as three,

and almost all Chinese children begin school by age five. Courses are similar to those in schools the world over, with a particular emphasis on citizenship and learning to work together. Yearly examinations begin in elementary school. After sixth grade, the more able students enter an academic secondary school; others begin vocational programs that include part-time work outside of school. The most able students are eventually sent to vocational colleges or academic universities at government expense. Local and provincial governments bear most of the cost of primary and secondary education. In poorer areas of the country, there is a shortage of good facilities, up-to-date textbooks, and trained staff.

Conditions are crowded in China's large university system, and most students have only enough money for the basic necessities. Yet a higher education is worth much sacrifice in a nation with a long tradition of respect for education. University graduates enjoy opportunities—and responsibilities—unknown to less gifted or fortunate people.

TRADITIONAL EMPLOYMENT

The vast majority of Chinese inherit their parents' way of life. In old China, a trade or job was called a person's "rice bowl." If a father earned his living as a farmer, a shoemaker, or a government official, it was likely that his son would pursue the same livelihood. In theory, a bright peasant lad could become a government official, but in reality very few could afford the education. Another lad might escape to the city to become a rickshaw puller, but he too would be the rare exception. For young women, the future was even more limited, their roles fixed by iron-bound tradition. Although opportunities are more varied today, the majority of people still inherit the "rice bowl."

Jobs in government-controlled industries are assigned by the government. Educated young people particularly resent the lack of freedom in choosing and changing jobs in the public sector. The rapid expansion of free enterprise in China has created jobs by the tens of millions. Government control of population movement has broken down as millions of people have migrated from the countryside to the cities in search of jobs or seasonal work.

A LACK OF MODERN TECHNOLOGY

Age-old methods and tools are more common than modern technology in China. Nowhere in the world are so many loads moved, so many fields plowed, and so many ditches dug with simple tools, raw muscle, and startling ingenuity. Most peasant families rely on wooden plows, hoes, rakes, barrels, and wheelbarrows; woven baskets, mats and fences; and pottery jars of every size and description. Horses, donkeys, and water buffalo are more common than tractors and trucks in the fields and on the roads of rural China.

Industrial development is hampered by a lack of modern technology. Miners, construction crews, and workers in such heavy industries as steelmaking have dirty, hard, and frequently dangerous jobs made even more difficult by the shortage of modern machinery. Workers in light industries, such as clothing and pottery manufacturing, labor in hot, stuffy, and poorly lit factories. Workers usually put in ten hours a day, five and a half or six days a week. However, Chinese workers have shown themselves to be quick learners, readily adapting to modern technologies as the tools become available.

With the decline in the birthrate, some population experts worry that China will have a serious shortage of working-age people to support a large elderly population in the second quarter of the twenty-first century. More optimistic experts predict that the introduction of modern technology and more efficient production methods will enable China to bridge the time when its population is out of balance.

LIVING STANDARDS

The average Chinese income is low by Western standards. Most families own little more than their clothing, bedding, cooking pots, a few tools, and two or three prized possessions. Until recently, most Chinese saved for the "four acquisitions": a wristwatch, a bicycle, a sewing machine, and a radio. With better economic conditions in the last decade, the list has evolved into "the eight bigs": an electric fan, a motorcycle, a refrigerator, a suite of furniture, a washing machine, a camera, a stereo, and a color television.

Everyday clothing styles are simple. Peasant farmers work in dark baggy pants and blouses, much as they have for centuries. City workers usually dress in white shirts or blouses and dark slacks or skirts. In the north and at higher elevations throughout China, heavily padded coats are needed to ward off the severe winter cold. Until recently, colorful clothing was frowned on by the Communist government, whose leaders usually wore gray "Mao jackets." However, changing attitudes and rising incomes are bringing grace and variety back to Chinese dress. China's leaders often appear in Western-style business suits when meeting foreign delegations, and young people are dressing more and more often in bright colors.

The daily diet is plain. In the south, people eat a great deal of rice—five or six bowls a day. Noodles are the staple in the north. The main meal of the day—at noon in the countryside and in the evening in the city—includes vegetables, soup, rice or noodles, and a small amount of pork, chicken, duck, or fish. Meat and vegetables are cut into tiny pieces, wasting nothing that can be eaten, and steamed or stir-fried in a wok. In different parts of the country, soy sauce, vinegar, garlic, mustard, ginger, hot peppers, and scallions are used to flavor the dishes. Banquets of a dozen or more courses mark special occasions, and their memory is savored for months afterward.

Green tea, the national drink, is consumed in steaming quantities even on the hottest days. Since few families have refrigerators, shopping is a daily chore. Each family receives coupons to buy the basic necessities at government stores. Most people prefer to buy other items in the free markets, where food is of better quality and prices can be negotiated. The danger of famine—the age-old curse of China—has receded in recent years, but the government admits that malnutrition remains a problem in poorer parts of the country.

MEDICAL CARE

The government of the PRC provides medical care free or at low cost to all citizens. Cultural tradition prizes moderation, and few Chinese abuse alcohol or drugs. Unfortunately, tobacco addiction is commonplace. Some major cities boast world-class hospitals and clinics. In rural China, where there is a shortage of medical facilities, an army of paramedics, called "barefoot doctors," treat minor ills and injuries.

About a third of China's doctors practice Western medicine, while the rest use traditional Chinese healing methods. The most famous traditional method is acupuncture. Ancient belief describes a system where the life-force, called t'chi, flows through the body along fourteen paths. If the t'chi is disturbed, the loss of balance between its negative side, the yin, and its positive side, the yang, causes illness. Inserting thin needles into several of the 800 acupuncture points on the body restores the balance and cures the patient. Dismissed as superstition in the West for centuries, acupuncture has gained respect in recent years, particularly for the treatment of pain. Modern research indicates that the needles affect the body's nervous system, blocking sensations from reaching the brain.

Herbal medicine has also gained wider respect in the West. Hundreds of herbal remedies are sold in China for the treatment of a variety of illnesses. Research has shown that many of these natural medicines work much like synthetic drugs produced in laboratories.

HOUSING AND PRIVACY

China has a severe housing shortage. In the cities, three generations of a family may share an apartment the size of an American living room. The government assigns housing, and the waiting list is long. A recently married couple may live for years with relatives before getting an apartment.

Outside the major cities, many homes lack electricity and running water. Water is drawn from a communal tap or pump, while kerosene lamps provide light. Some of the more modern rural districts have long rows of single-story apartments. Elsewhere, peasants have individual homes with two or three small rooms. The walls are built of mud bricks, and the few windows are often covered with paper rather than glass. In the north, where the winters are cold, the brick beds are heated from below with pipes running from the stove.

Privacy is a great luxury in much of China. In both urban and rural districts, several families often share a bathroom and a kitchen. Only through cooperation and patience can people accomplish routine chores. Arguments are community affairs, with neighbors gathering to listen and mediate. Considering the crowded conditions, it is remarkable that life goes on so smoothly.

Chinese tradition prizes cooperation and conformity to accepted social standards. China simply does not have room for over a billion rugged individualists. Good citizens keep their individuality within tight limits, and stubborn nonconformists are usually viewed as troublemakers. A phrase for the Chinese attitude entered English during World War II: "gung ho"—"work together."

An individual who violates community standards will be corrected by relatives, neighbors, schoolmates, or fellow workers. If this pressure produces no response, local authorities will step in, often forcing the nonconformist to submit to "public criticism" during a community or factory meeting.

The crime rate in China is considerably lower than in the industrialized West. Minor criminals risk fines, jail terms, and—perhaps worst of all—humiliation in the tight Chinese society. More serious offenders are sent to remote work camps. Violent criminals are sent to prison, while murderers, rapists, and those guilty of extreme corruption can be sentenced to public execution.

Despite its great size, its wealth of natural resources, and its vast pool of human labor and talent, China still lags far behind the United States and most Western nations in industrial development and living standards. The reasons lie in China's long, rich, and often tragic history.

2 The First Chinese

The prehistory of China is immeasurably long. *Homo erectus*, the probable ancestor of modern humans inhabited large areas of eastern China at least 400,000 years ago and probably many hundreds of thousands of years before that. *Homo erectus* eventually evolved into and was replaced by *Homo sapiens*, the immediate forebear of the modern human. Whether this evolution took place within or outside China is still unknown, but evidence of the presence of *Homo sapiens* in China dates back 50,000 and possibly 200,000 years. Somewhere between 50,000 and 120,000 years ago, *Homo sapiens* was replaced by *Homo sapiens sapiens*, the modern human. These ancestors of today's Chinese were Ice Age hunters and gatherers. They lived in small bands and migrated with the seasons in search of animals and ripening wild fruits and vegetables. Like early peoples everywhere, they feasted in times of plenty and went hungry in lean seasons.

The search for more reliable sources of food led to

the development of a primitive agriculture between 7,000 and 8,000 years ago. Some of the bands began seeding wild crops and domesticating small animals. As they devoted more of their time to farming, they spent less time wandering. They established permanent villages and joined other bands in larger tribal organizations. The Wei and Yellow river valleys of north central China proved especially suitable for this new way of life and became the cradle of Chinese civilization. In time, the farmers domesticated cattle and horses, developed techniques for making pottery and cloth, and learned how to raise better crops using fertilization and irrigation.

The success of agriculture produced a rapidly increasing population and the need for a stronger governmental system to keep peace and to promote cooperation. Chinese tradition says that the tribes of north central China were united about 2500 B.C. by a ruler named Huang Di (the Yellow Emperor). Huang Di and his wise counselors are credited with building the first cities, creating a code of laws, introducing public and religious ceremonies, and inventing the compass, the calendar, and a written language. Although no doubt embellished in the retelling, the stories of Huang Di's reign reveal an early yearning by the Chinese people for unity and stable government.

Sometime between 2200 and 1950 B.C., a heroic figure named the Emperor Yu answered that yearning by founding China's first ruling dynasty, the Xia. For the next 4,000 years, China was ruled by emperors who, on their death, handed over power to a chosen son or other close relative. Some of the dynasties sputtered and died in a few short decades, while others lasted for centuries.

Most of the history of the Xia dynasty, even its very existence, is clouded by myth. But we do know that in this period the people in the Yellow River basin built massive flood-control dikes, developed silk weaving,

began making fine pottery, adopted the use of bronze tools, and added several thousand characters to the written language.

WRITTEN HISTORY BEGINS

The cloud of myth begins to lift with the Shang dynasty, the first dynasty to leave written records. The Shang came to power somewhere between 1766 and 1576 B.C. The new dynasty established a class structure with a ruling class of hereditary nobles who ranked just below the emperor, an administrative class to maintain detailed records, and an artisan class to make beautiful possessions for the ruling classes. The majority of the people farmed the land, supporting the upper classes with their labor and taxes. The Shang rulers constructed cities surrounded by massive walls and built fine homes and palaces. Tool- and pottery-making, weaving, and writing became highly developed arts. Shang craftsmen cast beautiful bronze statues using techniques unequaled in Europe for another 2,500 years. Shang emperors were buried in large tombs with hoards of beautiful possessions and scores of human and animal sacrifices.

As was to happen over and over again in Chinese history, the Shang dynasty eventually lost energy and efficiency. The peasants and slaves at the lowest levels of society became resentful of the cruelty and extravagance of the rulers. Wars and official corruption drained the emperor's treasury. About 1027 B.C. (or as early as 1122 B.C.) the nobility of the state of Zhou led a rebellion against the Shang. According to legend, the last Shang emperor threw himself into the flames of his burning palace.

THE FEUDAL SYSTEM

The Zhou emperors established a feudal system, giving vast estates (or fiefdoms) to princes and nobles, who in turn were expected to contribute money, goods, sol-

diers, and laborers to the emperor. Aggressive princes extended China's borders outward into lands inhabited by "barbarian" peoples. Some of these powerful princes became virtually independent. Although the Zhou dynasty lasted for nine centuries, the longest dynasty in Chinese history, it often ruled in name only outside its capital in the Wei River valley.

Throughout the Zhou dynasty, the Chinese population grew rapidly as more and more land came under cultivation. Cities flourished, iron tools replaced bronze, crafts were refined to a high level, and trade spread far and wide. The late Zhou period produced a surge of interest in education, poetry, literature, and philosophy. Scholars and philosophers gained great esteem in Chinese society.

THE SEARCH FOR ANSWERS

The squabbles and ambitions of the feudal princes and petty kings in the late Zhou period worked against the welfare of the majority of Chinese. Reacting to the instability, scholar-philosophers developed philosophies for organizing a just and orderly society.

Daoism (Taoism) was based on the teachings of Laozi, a holy man who lived in the sixth century B.C. Daoists believed in putting aside earthly ambition and desire to seek harmony with the forces of nature. The ideal Daoist society would need few rules, since people living in harmony with nature would naturally live in harmony with one another. A kindly emperor would protect the people from want and strong passions with a minimum number of rules. Over the centuries, Daoism developed into a religion with many ceremonies, gods, and mystical practices.

The scholar and teacher Confucius (551?–479? B.C.) also wrestled with the problem of devising a system for a just and harmonious society. He emphasized education, individual self-discipline, and strict obedience to a

detailed code of conduct. Confucius laid out rules of address and behavior for each member of a Chinese family. Extending outward, the same rules gave everyone at every layer of Chinese society a code of behavior. In the ideal Confucian society, all people from the emperor to the poorest peasant would know their place and behave accordingly. Society would become stable and harmonious for all time. Although always more a philosophy than a religion, Confucianism's reverence for virtuous ancestors blended easily with Daoism's belief in many gods. Eventually, many Confucianists would conduct religious ceremonies honoring ancestors.

The Legalists made up a third school of thought. Unlike the followers of Confucius, who wanted to order society from the family outward, the Legalists wanted to impose order from the top down. They believed that the emperor should enact detailed and strict laws to cover nearly all aspects of behavior. Confronted with the prospect of harsh and certain punishment for disobedience, people would behave properly.

As different as they seem, Daoism, Confucianism, and Legalism each found a place in the Chinese view of the world. The Chinese celebrated their reverence for the natural world with Daoism, ordered family and social ethics according to Confucianism, and—for the most part—accepted Legalism's advice that a multitude of laws were needed to regulate society.

CHINA IS UNITED

By the third century B.C., Chinese civilization had spread over much of what is today eastern China. This vast, and by the standards of the time, heavily populated area was divided among seven feudal kings who paid little attention to the emperor of the decaying Zhou dynasty.

About 328 B.C., the aggressive rulers of the Qin kingdom in the Wei River valley set out to conquer the rest of China. The wars lasted more than a century and cost millions of lives. Without a strong dynasty to unite them against the Qin, the other six Zhou kingdoms fell one by one. In 246 B.C., the reigning king of Qin—a young man barely in his teens—declared himself Shi Huangdi, "the first emperor." By 221 B.C., he had conquered the last of his rivals and united China into a single centralized state.

Shi Huangdi (c. 259–209 B.C.) was one of history's great builders and also one of its great destroyers. Brilliant, cruel, greedy, and daring, he changed China for all time. As his armies marched out to conquer new territories, Shi Huangdi set about bringing order to his vast empire. On the advice of his Legalist ministers, he abolished the old feudal system and divided China into provinces under governors serving at his pleasure. Treachery, corruption, or poor performance by any official brought quick removal and, usually, execution.

Shi Huangdi built a dazzling new capital near Xi'an on the Yellow River. His palaces, shrines, gardens, roads, pools, and paths covered twenty-five square miles (65 sq. km). Luxury cost money, and the emperor's Legalist advisers furiously imposed new taxes to go along with laws covering nearly every aspect of Chinese life. Many of Shi Huangdi's reforms benefited the people. He decreed that all carts should be built with the same axle width so that they could travel easily along the empire's deeply rutted roads. He introduced a uniform system of weights and measures; standardized the empire's coinage; and issued a set of standard written characters.

Shi Huangdi stamped out opposition with ruthless efficiency. Anyone who criticized him or his Legalist advisers risked instant execution. He ordered the burning of books that might threaten his new order—a tragic act that destroyed much of China's written history, philosophy, poetry, and literature. He forbade discussion of the past, declaring that Chinese history was to begin with the Qin dynasty and its first emperor.

THE GREAT WALL

Shi Huangdi worried about invasion by the fierce tribes that wandered the forests and steppes beyond the northern border of his domain. He decided to construct a barrier against their raids on his settled, peaceable subjects. He connected a series of older walls to form a huge new wall. The Great Wall of China remains the largest construction project in history. Forty feet (12 m) high in places and wide enough for five horses to gallop abreast, it stretches some 1,500 miles (2,400 km) across northern China. Counting bends, dips, and branching walls, its total length exceeds 3,700 miles (5,960 km). Chinese tradition says that Shi Huangdi's wall took thirty years to complete and cost "a life for every stone."

Shi Huangdi died in 209 B.C. and was buried outside Xi'an in a magnificent underground tomb the size of a small city. (Although archaeologists have explored only a small portion of Shi Huangdi's tomb, they have already uncovered a remarkable army of life-size clay soldiers and horses.) Without its strong ruler, the Qin dynasty crumbled. Enraged by the brutality and greed of the dynasty, peasants and nobles joined forces to defeat the Qin armies. The victorious nobles attempted to restore the feudal system, but the common people resisted a return to the bad old days. In 202 B.C., the great peasant leader Liu Bang defeated the last of his opponents to unite China under a new dynasty built on the ruins of the Qin.

Despite its short life, the Qin dynasty changed China in extraordinary ways. The political system established by Shi Huangdi would survive in much the same form until the twentieth century.

3 Emperors, Dynasties, and Mandarins

In 202 B.C., Liu Bang became the first emperor of the Han dynasty. Although a person of little education, he was a shrewd ruler. He awarded land to his generals and to those nobles who had sided with him, but he kept their fiefdoms small and weak by surrounding them with large provinces under the control of royal governors.

The emperors who followed Liu Bang carefully chipped away at the power of the noble class. In 144 B.C., the Emperor Xiao Jing decreed that every lord must will his lands in equal parts to all his sons, rather than following a practice called primogeniture that left the entire fiefdom to the eldest. This clever decree so divided the wealth of the nobility that within two or three generations they became little more than minor landlords unable to threaten the power of the emperor.

The Han emperors courted the loyalty of the scholar class. Confucian scholars had originally opposed the concentration of power in the hands of a central government (the policy of the Legalists). But the Han emperors wooed them with rich appointments, prestige, and a willingness to listen. Soon the Confucian scholars became the imperial system's strongest backers.

THE MANDARINS

The Han emperors recruited the governing officials of the empire from the scholar class. Candidates spent long years studying the Confucian texts to learn the principles of good government and a harmonious society. When in their late twenties or early thirties, candidates felt ready to tackle the rigorous government examinations. The examinations were a test of both physical and mental stamina. Locked in tiny cubicles for days on end, some candidates went mad or committed suicide. Others did so poorly that they were given only minor positions as clerks and tax collectors. But those who emerged with high scores could look forward to careers of wealth and power.

A scholar who achieved one of the nine highest levels in the examinations could adopt the dress and title of a mandarin. The mandarins were a remarkable class of scholar-officials. Unlike any other ruling class in the world, they held their positions not because of inherited wealth or blood ties to the royal family but because of their intelligence and education. In theory, a young man from the lowest class could become a mandarin if he had the brains and energy to master the knowledge needed to pass the examinations. Some succeeded, but the expense of getting the necessary education kept most young men—no matter how bright—out of the mandarin class.

The mandarins became indispensable to the day-to-day governing of the vast empire. Although dynasties rose and fell, the mandarins maintained their power for more than 2,000 years.

THE IMPERIAL HOUSEHOLD

Intelligent and energetic emperors kept a careful watch on the great web of administration extending from the imperial court to the smallest and most distant village in the land. Part of an emperor's power came from the awe he inspired as the "reigning son of heaven." The Chinese believed a dynasty ruled with divine approval—the "mandate of heaven." If a dynasty ruled well, it might remain in power for centuries. But if it ruled poorly, the mandate of heaven would be "withdrawn" and the dynasty overthrown.

Emperors spent their lives surrounded with innumerable luxuries and armies of servants. Yet the constant work of reading and signing documents, consulting with senior ministers, and performing state and religious ceremonies, taxed the emperor's life. Intrigue and jealousy plagued the court, and the constant danger of assassination haunted the emperors.

Emperors had twenty or thirty wives and many more concubines—women who provided the emperor with sexual companionship without the legal formality of marriage. The women's apartments were a center of intrigue as wives and concubines competed to gain the emperor's favor. Although the first wife might expect her eldest son to become the next "son of heaven," his position was by no means assured as other wives tried to bring their sons' virtues to the emperor's attention. Women who gained favor could persuade an emperor to appoint their fathers, uncles, brothers, and nephews to high positions as ministers and generals. Weak or child emperors often became mere figureheads controlled by powerful families.

To protect the purity of the royal line, only castrated males, called eunuchs, were employed as servants inside the Forbidden City. Through their daily contact with the imperial family, some eunuchs gained great influence. Quite naturally, they became the enemies of the senior mandarins who had qualified for positions through the examination system.

THE CLASS SYSTEM

Traditional Chinese society was rather like a spider's web, with the emperor and his family at the center and the rest of the people occupying bands radiating outward in ever-widening circles. The band nearest the center was occupied by the senior mandarins and their competitors for influence: the court eunuchs and the relatives of wives or concubines who enjoyed the emperor's favor. Lesser mandarins occupied the next band outward, while non-mandarin officials (tax collectors, clerks, inspectors, teachers, and the like) occupied the rays of the web extending to its outer extremities, where some minor officials were very poor.

The first band beyond the inner government circles was occupied by wealthy landlords, merchants, manufacturers, shipowners, and mine operators, whose riches gave them considerable influence. Rich peasant farmers, who rented most of their land to others or hired laborers to work it, occupied the next band. They lived comfortable lives and exerted political influence on the local level. Artisans, craft workers, shopkeepers, junior army officers, doctors, moneylenders, monks, nuns, and the practitioners of innumerable other trades lived on the next band, where riches were less abundant.

The vast majority of the Chinese people occupied the wide middle bands. First came the so-called middle peasants, who owned all or most of their land, perhaps renting a few extra acres from a wealthy landlord when they could afford it. Next came the poor peasants, who had to rent almost all their land or work on the farms of others. All told, nine out of ten Chinese lived on these two wide bands far from the wealth and power concentrated in the narrow rings close to the center. The poor peasants lived hard lives of grinding labor in all seasons, forever at the mercy of the weather, bandits, and the rich landlords who owned most of the land. When crops failed, millions of peasants starved, and even in good times extreme thrift was a necessary virtue for the majority of Chinese.

Common soldiers and sailors (held in low esteem in Chinese society and paid little), laborers, peddlers, rickshaw pullers, and other landless workers occupied the next to the last band. On the outermost band lived the humblest citizens of all: butchers, hide tanners, prostitutes, dung collectors, wandering actors and singers, and the practitioners of other spurned or "unclean" occupations. Outside the web entirely were the castoffs of society: beggars, lepers, pickpockets, thieves, and bandits.

THE MIDDLE KINGDOM

The Chinese considered their country and civilization the most advanced in the world. For them, China was the "Middle Kingdom," a land located at the center of the world and surrounded by crude, uncivilized peoples they called barbarians. To protect the northern border of China, the Han emperors completed the Great Wall, and it was repaired and rebuilt down through the centuries by succeeding dynasties. The Great Wall was not a perfect barrier against invading armies, but it served as a symbol of China's determination to keep the outside world at a distance.

The ancient Chinese had many reasons to consider their civilization the greatest in the world. They made cast iron 1,500 years before Europeans did. They invented papermaking, gunpowder, silk weaving, the magnetic compass, and the printing press. China's scientists made major discoveries in mathematics, astronomy, zoology, and other sciences. China's artists painted pictures of wondrous beauty, and its writers composed superb novels and poems. Its artisans produced exquisite objects of every description for the royal family and the wealthy classes.

Many of the emperors were wise, just, and humane. Recognizing that hungry people made unruly subjects, they maintained huge granaries to feed the people in times of want. They harnessed the muscle power of the Chinese people in immense public-works projects for the benefit of the populace and for the greater glory of China. With simple tools and strong backs, the ancient Chinese built the largest system of canals, flood-control dikes, and defensive walls in history. With considerable reason, the Middle Kingdom could claim to have the greatest cities, the most glorious palaces, and the strongest fortresses on earth. Only the Roman Empire, coming into its glory about the same time as the Han dynasty, could rival the boast.

CHINA DIVIDED

Except for one brief interruption, the Han dynasty ruled China for more than 400 years. But like dynasties before and after, the Han dynasty eventually ran out of energy. Corrupt eunuchs within the palace took control of the government, raising taxes, selling appointments for cash, and executing many honest mandarins on trumped-up charges. In A.D. 184, a great rebellion swept central China. Disgusted generals found that they could not wage effective war because the eunuchs had pilfered the military budget, sold supplies, and even taken bribes from the rebels. When the Han emperor died in A.D. 189, leaving no clear successor, the generals turned against the eunuchs. Thirty years of war followed as rival generals tried to gain control of the government. Eventually, China was divided into three kingdoms: the Wei in the north, the Wu in the south, and Shu-Han in the southwest.

The Three Kingdoms period was filled with hardship for the common people. Almost constant wars ravaged the land. Hostile tribes from north of the Great Wall conquered large areas once ruled by the Han dynasty. Dikes, canals, and roads decayed. Imperial granaries stood empty. Yet the Chinese people persisted through all the hardships, always believing that China would someday be unified again.

Many Chinese sought comfort in a religion new to China: Buddhism. Like Daoism, Buddhism called on the believer to put aside worldly ambitions and desires. The first principle of Buddhism is that life is suffering—a concept borne out frequently in Chinese daily life. All living beings were doomed to ride the "wheel of life" through endless cycles of birth, growth, maturity, aging, illness, and death unless they sought the enlightenment of Buddhism. Through long contemplation and denial of temptation, a person could achieve a state of perfection called Nirvana, where the self ceased to have importance and the believer could step off the endlessly repeating wheel of reincarnation.

Although occasionally suppressed by emperors jealous of the wealth amassed by worldly Buddhist monasteries, Buddhism survived to take its place in the assortment of beliefs accepted—often simultaneously—by the common people.

THE SUI AND THE TANG

China was briefly reunified in 589 A.D. by the Sui dynasty. Like the Qin dynasty nearly eight centuries before, the Sui accomplished much in a short time. Their greatest achievement was the construction of the Grand Canal for the shipping of rice from the fertile south to the arid north. Eventually stretching some

1,050 miles (1,700 km) from Hangzhou to Beijing, the Grand Canal remains the longest canal ever built. But forced labor on the canal and the bloody cost of an unsuccessful war to conquer Korea earned the Sui the hatred of the people. Less than thirty years after coming to power, the Sui lost the mandate of heaven.

As rebellions again swept the land, a remarkable young man named Li Shimin (A.D. 601–649) convinced his father, a provincial official, to make a bid for power. In a seven-year campaign at the head of his father's army, Li Shimin reunified China under the Tang dynasty. After his father's death, Li Shimin reigned as the emperor T'ai Tsung from A.D. 627 to 649. Perhaps the greatest emperor in Chinese history, he used his extraordinary skills as a scholar, administrator, and soldier to weld China into the world's largest and richest empire.

After Li Shimin's death, his good-natured but lazy successor, the emperor Gao Zong, let his wife Wu Chao (A.D. 624–705) take charge of the empire. The empress Wu governed with great skill through her loyal and capable mandarins until forced by illness and age to give up power a few months before her death. After the brief reign of her weak son, her grandson, the emperor Xuan Zong, became the third great Tang ruler. During his long reign (A.D. 712–756), the Tang empire reached its height. While Europe suffered through the grim decades of the early Middle Ages, a China at peace achieved spectacular growth in wealth and learning.

Near the end of Xuan Zong's reign, an ambitious general led a massive revolt against the emperor. The devastating cost of putting down the uprising tilted the Tang dynasty into a century-long decline. Power passed gradually into the hands of regional governors, who only occasionally bothered to express loyalty to the emperor. In A.D. 868, another military rebellion tipped China into chaos. The civil war lasted nearly forty years, destroying the ancient capital of Xi'an and finally driving the Tang dynasty from power in A.D. 907.

The cycle of Chinese history had turned again. The regional governors discarded even their casual loyalty to the central government and declared their states independent. In the north, rival generals fought for the throne of the Tang dynasty. Over the next half century, five dynasties came and went, none of them able to control more than a third of the area once governed by the Tang dynasty.

THE RELUCTANT EMPEROR

To the majority of Chinese, the Five Dynasties period seemed a tremendous step backward. The people longed for a leader who would restore the unity, peace, and glory of earlier times. Their hopes were finally fulfilled by Zhao Kuangyin (A.D. 927–976), a general in the army of the last of the five short-lived dynasties. One night in A.D. 960, the general was jolted awake by a group of his own soldiers entering his tent with drawn swords. He was, they announced, the new emperor whether he liked it or not.

Zhao Kuangyin's soldiers distrusted the empress who was ruling for the recently crowned infant emperor. At first unwilling, but with a growing sense of destiny, Zhao Kuangyin led his army into the capital of Kaifeng. He did not act like earlier generals who had come to overthrow an emperor and install a new dynasty. He spared the lives of the royal family and invited the government's best ministers to work for his newly declared Song dynasty. Next, the new emperor called his generals together and announced that to prevent further military uprisings, he was offering them all lavish retirements in exchange for their letters of resignation. They all agreed.

With his base secure, Zhao Kuangyin called on the governors of the independent provinces to join him in restoring unity to China. Impressed by his wisdom and mercy, all but a few agreed. Those who chose to resist found that they could not count on their armies to fight very hard against the popular new emperor. Three years after Zhao Kuangyin's death in A.D. 976, his brother, the new emperor, brought the last of the rebellious provinces under the rule of the Song dynasty.

THE PEACEABLE SONG

The successors of Zhao Kuangyin governed the Middle Kingdom with great skill. They expanded the mandarin civil service and reduced the power of the army. Just and efficient government kept China peaceful, and the Song dynasty was never threatened by the internal revolts that had plagued earlier dynasties. The Song rulers made peace with the aggressive nomad tribes along China's northern border in 1004, even though this meant that the Song dynasty would never hold sway over as much territory as the Tang dynasty had in its glory.

For over a century, China was at peace. The population expanded rapidly as the people prospered under benevolent taxes and laws. If crops failed or if floods washed away months of work, the government moved quickly to assist the peasants. In the cities and at court, artists, writers, and philosophers worked with renewed zest. Many Chinese in later centuries would look back on the Song period as China's golden age. But it was an age that could not last as the Middle Kingdom's riches beckoned to the restless, nomadic peoples of the north.

4 Invaders from the North

Chinese emperors built and maintained the Great Wall to keep the fierce nomadic tribes of Mongolia and Manchuria at bay. But for all its scale and grandeur, the Great Wall could never withstand a determined invasion. In the confused period following the fall of the Tang dynasty in A.D. 907, the Khitan people of southern Mongolia occupied an area of northeastern China on either side of the Great Wall. In 1004, the Song dynasty tried to retake the territory between Beijing and the wall, but the peaceable Song never had a talent for war and soon gave up the attempt.

The Chinese and the Khitans lived in peace for more than a century. Under the influence of Chinese civilization, the Khitans abandoned their nomadic ways for a more settled life in an independent state they named Liao. With their warrior traditions forgotten, they were ill-prepared to meet an invasion by another Mongolian people, the Jurchen (Kin) Tartars. The Jurchen cavalry swept through a breach in the wall and

48

smashed the Khitan army in 1124. The Song emperor of China tried to take advantage of the fighting by sending an army to occupy a piece of territory near the wall, but only succeeded in angering the Jurchen. The poorly trained and long unused Song army was no match for the hardy, warlike nomads. With the Jurchen cavalry sweeping down on the Song capital of Kaifeng, the emperor quit the throne in favor of his son.

The new emperor quickly agreed to a truce, but unwise advisers encouraged him to attack as the Jurchen army began withdrawing. It was a disastrous blunder. The enraged Jurchen launched an all-out invasion of China. They captured Kaifeng and then pushed south, scattering the remains of the Song armies. A capable Song general finally stopped the Jurchen army below the Yangzi. In 1141, the Chinese and the Jurchen made peace. The Song gave up seven northern provinces—all of China north of the Huai River. For the next century, the Song governed central and southern China from the city of Hangzhou, but in this new era of peace, they forgot the lessons of war.

North of the Huai River, the Chinese outnumbered their Jurchen conquerors several times over. Like the Khitans before them, the Jurchen quickly lost their nomadic identity. Within decades, they were all but absorbed into the Chinese population and culture. The Jurchen rulers had become another Chinese dynasty, hoping that the Great Wall would protect them from northern invaders. But a hurricane of devastation unlike anything the world had ever known was building in the cold, windswept grasslands of Mongolia.

THE COMING OF THE MONGOLS

Temujin (1162?–1227), probably history's greatest conqueror and one of its greatest butchers, was born into the family of a Mongol chieftain. His father was murdered by rivals when Temujin was thirteen, forcing the family to flee onto the harsh Mongolian plain. They survived, and Temujin's deeds of cunning and courage won him a band of devoted followers. He reclaimed his father's chieftainship and then set out to conquer all the Mongol tribes. In thirty years of almost continuous warfare, Temujin destroyed his rivals and united the Mongols into a single incredibly warlike people. Proclaimed Jenghiz (Genghis) Khan—"universal king"— by his fellow chieftains in 1206, he prepared his Mongol hordes for a conquest that would create the largest land empire in history.

Rapid population growth and a long warrior tradition gave Jenghiz Khan a huge and experienced army. All Mongol males were soldiers from adolescence to old age. Conditioned by the harsh climate of their homeland, they could travel 100 miles (160 km) a day on their small, sturdy horses. At a gallop, a Mongol warrior could shoot his short, powerful bow with amazing accuracy, the arrows striking with enough force to penetrate armor.

In 1210, Jenghiz Khan invaded the Jurchen domain of northern China. The Jurchen called on the Song dynasty for help, but the Song ignored their pleas and warnings. The Mongols raped, burned, and pillaged their way through the cradle of Chinese civilization along the Yellow River. Any city that resisted was leveled, all its inhabitants slaughtered or enslaved. Leaving generals to finish the conquest of northern China, Jenghiz Khan struck westward. By 1223, his hordes had swept across Central Asia and Persia and into European Russia. In 1224, Jenghiz Khan returned to the East. He fell on the Xixia kingdom in northwestern China, an area that had been ruled by Tibetan conquerors since the decline of the Tang dynasty more than three centuries before. The Mongols laid waste to the cities, slaughtered nearly every man, woman, and child, and left the once-prosperous Xixia kingdom a wilderness.

What was left of the Jurchen empire of northern China lay open to the hordes of the Great Khan. The Mongols looked on the settled, irrigated farmlands of the Chinese with disgust. One chieftain stated the common opinion: "Although we have conquered the Chinese, they are of no use to us. It would be better to exterminate them entirely, and let the grass grow so that we can have grazing land for our horses."

Fortunately for the Chinese, a remarkable man had the courage to offer a different plan. Yelu Qucai was a descendant of the Khitan royal family and a great admirer of Chinese civilization. Captured by the Mongols, he had saved his life by agreeing to become an adviser to the Khan. He convinced Jenghiz Khan that it made more sense to tax the captured Chinese provinces than to lay them to waste. (Later Yelu Qucai played on Mongol superstitions to make them abandon their invasion of India. Perhaps no one in history saved more lives or did more to rescue great civilizations than the cunning, courageous Yelu Qucai. Yet his name is nearly forgotten, while many remember the name of Jenghiz Khan, perhaps the greatest destroyer in history.)

Jenghiz Khan died in 1227. His son Ogedei (1185–1241) completed the conquest of the Jurchen empire but, following Yelu Qucai's advice, spared the country the worst of the Mongol savagery. The Song emperor of south China concluded an uneasy alliance with Ogedei, and the Mongols again turned their attention to conquering the West. Ogedei's hordes defeated the Russian princes, stormed through Poland and Hungary, and were on the brink of invading western Europe when he died in 1241. The problem of who would be the next khan sent the Mongol generals rushing home to cast their votes. Western Europe was saved.

After two lesser figures briefly held the khanship, Jenghiz Khan's grandson and Ogedei's nephew Möngke (1208–1259) became Great Khan in 1248. Intent on equaling the conquests of his grandfather, Möngke sent his brother Hulegu to invade the Muslim Middle East, while he set out to conquer the Song empire. Hulegu captured Baghdad in modern Iraq in 1258 and pushed on through Syria to within striking distance of the sacred city of Jerusalem. But once again news from the East saved one of the great cradles of civilization: Möngke had died, his conquest of Song China barely begun. Hulegu withdrew from Syria, leaving behind a portion of his army. On September 3, 1260, an Egyptian army destroyed the Mongol army at the battle of Ain Jalut near the Sea of Galilee, wrecking the fiction of Mongol invincibility and ending forever the westward push of the Mongol empire.

Song China was not as lucky. Kubilai, youngest son of Ogedei, renewed the invasion of southern China. His armies pushed steadily south until, in 1279, the last Song emperor threw himself into the sea rather than surrender. For the first time since the fall of the Tang dynasty in A.D. 907, China was unified under a single ruler. Kubilai chose Beijing as the capital of his Yuan dynasty. Like invaders before them, the Mongols adopted many Chinese attitudes and customs. The Yuan dynasty employed the mandarins of the fallen Song dynasty to collect the taxes and to administer China. Chinese artisans made the splendors of Kubilai's court, while Chinese poets sang of its unparalleled glory. Beyond the palace walls, the Chinese people provided the muscle, brains, and energy needed to satisfy the appetites of the invaders.

END OF THE MONGOL TERROR

At its height, the Mongol empire stretched across Asia from the Pacific Ocean to the shores of the Mediterranean. But it was a fragile empire built on a foundation of military skill and raw terror, and it soon buckled under its own weight. By the 1290s, the empire had split into four separate realms. Kubilai, although in title the Great Khan, received only polite homage from the rulers of the other three khanates. Kubilai's descendants fought over the throne of China for half a century after his death in 1294.

Seething under the indignities heaped on them by the Mongols, the Chinese people rebelled in 1348. A peasant-born Buddhist monk and sometime bandit named Zhu Yuanzhang (1328–1399) led a large rebel army in a campaign that pushed the Mongols steadily northward. In 1360, he declared himself emperor, announcing that the new Ming dynasty would rule from the great walled city of Nanjing. In 1382, Ming forces drove the last of the Mongols beyond the Great Wall. The Ming victory opened an era of great power and prosperity for China. Zhu Yuanzhang's successor, the Yongle Emperor (1360–1424), moved the capital back to Beijing and employed 200,000 workers to build a huge complex of palaces at its heart. For centuries, the Forbidden City would be off-limits to all but the most select Chinese ministers and the most prestigious foreign dignitaries.

Unlike many emperors before and most who would follow, Yongle had no fear of the outside world. He reopened the ancient caravan routes stretching across Asia to Arabia and Europe. He sent naval expeditions to explore and trade along the coasts of Japan, Indonesia, Indochina, India, Persia, Arabia, and the east coast of Africa. His military expeditions reclaimed all the land lost to the empire since the fall of the Tang in A.D. 907.

In the decades following Yongle's death, the Ming dynasty fell into the age-old pattern of decline and decay. The Tibetans, Mongols, and Vietnamese all defeated Chinese military expeditions. Pirate fleets cruised the coastal waters, capturing trading vessels and raiding ports. Japan, unified after centuries of clan warfare, landed armies in Korea and on China's north-east coast. The Ming spent colossal sums meeting these threats. Although it was the richest country in the world, not even the prosperous Middle Kingdom could afford the cost. The Ming abandoned the rebellious frontier territories and most of their overseas trade.

THE LAST DYNASTY BEGINS

In the early 1600s, a new danger emerged as the Manchus, an aggressive Manchurian people related to the Jurchen Tartars, began challenging the power of the Ming along China's northern frontier. The overextended Ming armies retreated behind the Great Wall. Meanwhile, the cities of the south grew restless as the corrupt Ming government laid heavier and heavier taxes on the people to support the cost of defending China's borders.

As unpaid troops mutinied or deserted, an adventurer from the northwest, Li Zhicheng, led a rebel army toward Beijing. Caught between the threat of the Manchus on the north and Li Zhicheng on the west, the last Ming emperor hanged himself in the spring of 1644. A victorious Li Zhicheng entered Beijing to declare a new dynasty. He probably would have succeeded except for the personal hatred of Wu Sangui, the Ming general charged with defending the Great Wall. Wu opened the wall to the Manchus and then hunted down the fleeing Li Zhicheng, while the Manchu army occupied Beijing without a fight.

For the next eighteen years, Wu Sangui fought for control of southern China against various contenders for the Ming throne. Meanwhile, the devout Shunzhi, first emperor of the Manchu Qing dynasty, ruled the north quietly and without much skill or interest. In 1661, he either died or—according to Chinese tradition—abandoned his throne for the religious life of a monastery. The new emperor was a boy of eight under the control of uncles and court eunuchs. He would eventually free himself to become one of the outstanding emperors in Chinese history, the great Kangxi (1653–1723).

As Kangxi grew to manhood, China south of the Yangzi was divided into three realms governed by princes supposedly answering to the Manchu court but rarely paying it much mind. One of the princes was the formidable old soldier Wu Sangui, who neither liked nor feared the Manchus and their young emperor. In 1673, Wu Sangui threw off his allegiance to the Manchus, marching from his base in the southwest with the intention of overthrowing the dynasty and claiming the throne for his descendants. But Kangxi was no longer a boy. He won over the other princes of southern China, defeated Wu Sangui's Mongol allies, and turned back the old soldier. When Wu Sangui died preparing for another campaign, Kangxi launched an invasion of the southwest. Even though the other princes of southern China had sided with him against Wu Sangui, Kangxi quickly deposed them to prevent further rebellions. His army captured the rebel capital of the Wu family in 1682, exterminated the last of its members, and brought all of China under the direct rule of the Manchus.

Kangxi was followed by other capable emperors, as China prospered for a century under the strict but efficient Qing dynasty. The dynasty's armies conquered Tibet, Mongolia, and Taiwan. Within China, the Manchus kept the people under tight control by stationing garrisons in all major cities. Like foreign dynasties before them, the Manchus depended on the Chinese mandarin class to administer the vast empire. However, unlike earlier invaders who had adopted Chinese customs, the Manchus kept much of their own identity. Manchu men wore their hair unbraided, while native Chinese men were forced to shave the front of the scalp and wear their remaining hair in a tightly bound braid, called a queue, as a sign of abject submission. Manchu women did not follow the ancient Chinese custom of foot-binding—tightly bandaging the feet from infancy on to produce abnormally small feet, thought beautiful by Han men. The "large" feet of Manchu women discouraged intermarriage between the Manchus and the Han Chinese and preserved the ethnic identity of the Manchus.

Although they disdained many Chinese ways, the early Manchu rulers were generous patrons of China's arts, scholarship, and philosophy. Under the Qing, painters, writers, and calligraphers produced works of great refinement. Royal workshops turned out porcelain of a beauty unexcelled in any age. Scholars assembled monumental encyclopedias, dictionaries, and geographies to bring together more than 2,000 years of Chinese learning. Philosophers combed ancient Confucian texts in pursuit of a perfect understanding of human character and interaction.

With the beginning of the 1800s, however, the energy of the dynasty began to seep away. Corruption became widespread despite the efforts of many officials of honesty and good conscience. Wealthy landlords charged exorbitant rents, forcing tens of millions of peasants to live in lifelong poverty. When epidemics, floods, and famines ravaged the countryside, the Qing did little to relieve the distress of the peasants. The harsh conditions led to frequent rebellions that kept much of China in turmoil for years on end.

As the Qing dynasty decayed, aggressive foreigners began eyeing China's riches. But these were not other Asians with at least some respect for Chinese culture, but white-skinned Westerners with strange ways, fearsome weapons, and often an open disdain for the Chinese. Not since the Mongol invasion six centuries before had Chinese civilization faced such a colossal challenge.

5 A Collision of Cultures

Neither the Great Wall nor the harsh edicts of emperors could keep China isolated from the outside world. Inevitably, the "barbarians" came calling, greedy for Chinese spices, tea, porcelain, and—above all—silk. According to Chinese legend, the empress Si Lingji, wife of the Yellow Emperor Huang Di (c. 2,500 B.C.), first discovered how the cocoons of the mulberry silk moth could be woven into a luxurious fabric. For the next 3,000 years, the craft remained a state secret, protected by the threat of execution for anyone who whispered a word outside the imperial shops.

The first silk reached the Mediterranean world between the sixth and seventh centuries B.C. Sensationally popular with wealthy Greeks and Romans, silk commanded incredible prices, becoming worth—quite literally—its weight in gold. To meet the demand, intrepid Arab, Turkish, and Persian traders created the Silk Route, a meandering trail stretching from Syria across 4,000 miles (6,500 km) of plains, mountains, and deserts to the fabled Middle Kingdom. The traders traveled by camel caravan in journeys that often took years and that only the fortunate survived.

For centuries the Silk Route provided the only link between Europe and China. A fabulous folklore about the Middle Kingdom grew up in the West, dispelled only occasionally by eyewitness reports brought back by the handful of European missionaries who dared to travel the dangerous road to the East. About A.D. 550, two priests bribed by the Byzantine emperor Justinian (483–565) smuggled silkworm eggs and the seeds of mulberry trees from China to Constantinople (modern Istanbul, Turkey) in a hollow staff. Westerners successfully cultivated the silkworm, but Chinese silk remained an exotic luxury.

During the Middle Ages, hostile Chinese emperors or wars in central Asia closed the Silk Route for decades at a time. Yet the treasures of the mysterious Middle Kingdom continued to beckon. Late in the thirteenth century, the Venetian trader Marco Polo took the Silk Route to China, where he spent seventeen years in the employ of the Mongol emperor Kubilai Khan. Some years after returning to Italy in 1295, Polo dictated an account of his adventures. Although *The Travels of Marco Polo* contained much inaccurate hearsay about the history of the Middle Kingdom, it remained Europe's chief source of information about China for more than two centuries.

In the early 1500s, Portuguese trading ships began reaching China by way of a long, dangerous voyage around the southern tip of Africa. In 1557, the reigning Ming emperor allowed the Portuguese to build a trading post at Macao, about 75 miles (120 km) south of Canton. By the mid-1600s, ships from many nations were trading at Macao, Canton, and the other ports of southern China. They brought the best the West had to offer, but found the Chinese interested in little from the barbarian lands except silver, gold, and Arabian horses.

As the number of Western traders increased over the next two centuries, the Chinese emperors became nervous about the influence of the Europeans, particularly the Christian missionaries who often accompanied the traders. In 1757, at the height of the Manchu Qing dynasty, the Emperor Qianlong confined all foreign merchants to Macao and Canton. When the Western nations objected, he dismissed their requests for open trade with the haughty reply that China already "possessed all things in prolific abundance."

THE OPIUM TRADE

The growing demand for Chinese products created a dangerous balance-of-trade problem for the West. The flood of silver pouring into China produced a shortage of hard currency in Europe and America. But in the late 1700s, the British found a new commodity for the China trade: the powerful narcotic drug opium. British ships from India began bringing opium into Canton in large shipments. The river of silver reversed direction, and China began to feel the economic pinch.

The medicinal uses of opium had been known in China for centuries, but the scarcity of supply had kept the price high and only a few people in the wealthy classes smoked opium for pleasure. The British importation of large amounts of opium slashed the price, and soon many Chinese in the working classes became addicts. For a few cents a person could smoke a pipe of opium and forget the backbreaking labor of the long days. But the drug left the smoker depressed, lethargic, and craving another pipe.

Recognizing the threat to the economy and the health of the people, the Chinese government tried to stamp out the opium trade. Courts ordered the execution of drug dealers and sentenced opium smokers to whippings and the public humiliation of wearing a heavy wooden collar called the *canque*. But British traders refused to abandon their profitable business.

They anchored heavily armed ships in the bay below Canton and continued selling opium to Chinese smugglers. In 1839, Chinese troops seized and destroyed a huge shipment of opium.

Foreign traders who refused to allow inspection of their goods were blockaded inside their warehouses until they cooperated. Outraged by these "attacks" on its citizens, Britain dispatched a powerful fleet to punish China. The Chinese had few warships and almost no modern weapons. The British quickly captured Shanghai, Nanjing, and a half dozen other cities, forcing the emperor to sue for peace.

The British demanded harsh terms. China paid a huge fine; opened the ports of Xiamen, Fuzhou, Ningbo, and Shanghai to foreign trade; and ceded the island of Hong Kong to Britain. As the British began building Hong Kong into one of the world's richest trading centers, other Western powers rushed to force treaties on the defeated dynasty. The Chinese gave in to demands for "extraterritoriality," the right of the Western powers to establish self-governing enclaves in the newly opened treaty ports. Western administrators, judges, and imported troops and police would enforce Western laws and customs within these "concession areas." In addition, any Westerner accused of breaking the law anywhere in China would be tried not in a local Chinese court but in a Western court in a concession area. Chinese gangs moved their headquarters into the concession areas, where they could organize their far-flung criminal activities beyond the reach of Chinese law. Western authorities looked the other way or openly collaborated with the gangsters.

BLOODY REBELLIONS

The humiliation of the Qing dynasty at the hands of the Westerners set the Chinese masses seething. The Manchu emperors had never been popular, and many Chinese felt that the dynasty had lost the mandate of heaven. Rebellions broke out across China. For years, rebels—some no more than common bandits—controlled large sections of rural China.

In the late 1840s, a strange and magnetic man took advantage of the unrest to launch the largest rebellion in Chinese history. Hong Xiuquan (1813–1864) was a member of the Hakka minority of southern China. His family had made sacrifices to prepare him for the government examinations that would give him a secure place in the civil service. But Hong repeatedly failed the examinations. Despondent, he fell ill. In a fever, he had a vision of a golden-haired man who called him younger brother. Some years later, while working as a village schoolteacher, Hong read a Christian missionary pamphlet and thought he recognized the golden-haired man as Jesus Christ.

Hong became a passionate convert to Christianity, spreading the religion he only sketchily understood among the peasants and miners of Guangxi province. Hong's Society of God Worshipers grew with astonishing speed. The God Worshipers tore down "pagan" temples, denounced the rigid Confucian principles that governed Chinese society, and drilled in preparation for a war to drive the hated Manchus back into the "wilderness" beyond the Great Wall. In the rugged Thistle Mountain region of eastern Guangxi, Hong set up a social organization unlike anything China had ever seen. Men and women were segregated; living, working, and drilling in separate organizations. Alcohol and opium were forbidden. Believers gave all their money and valuables to the common treasury. All land was also held in common, with each family working according to their abilities and receiving according to their needs. In this respect particularly, Hong's followers practiced a socialist principle that would later become one of the central ideals of communism in China and the Soviet Union.

The growing number and militancy of Hong's followers finally attracted the attention of the lethargic government. In December 1850, a Qing army advanced on Hong's mountain stronghold, only to be soundly defeated by the God Worshipers. In the flush of victory, Hong declared himself Taiping Tianguo—"the Emperor of Great Peace from the Heavenly Kingdom"—a title that gave his followers their common name, the Taiping. The Taiping army marched out of the mountains to overthrow the Qing dynasty. After some early failures, the rebels pushed north with a series of extraordinary victories. As city after city fell, tens of thousands of converts flocked to Hong's banner. In March 1854, Hong captured the great city of Nanjing. His followers butchered 40,000 Manchu men, women, and children in a terrible revenge on the "devils" from north of the Great Wall.

If Hong had continued his march north toward Beijing, he probably would have driven the Qing dynasty from power. But he let the chance slip away. Instead, he lived in luxury among his concubines, while searching the Bible for references to his "mission." Several of his most able advisers engaged in a power struggle and were either assassinated or fled Nanjing. Many Chinese who had viewed the Taiping rebels as freedom fighters were horrified by their attacks on traditional religious symbols and Confucian standards. Many Westerners—particularly in the missionary community—at first sympathized with the Taiping cause, but became disenchanted when they learned about the more bizarre aspects of Hong's faith and Taiping social organization. Western business interests preferred to deal with the weak Qing dynasty rather than a possible Taiping dynasty that would carry out Hong's promise to destroy the opium trade and to end extraterritorial rights in the treaty ports.

As dedicated mandarin generals rallied the Qing armies, the Western powers dispatched gunboats and military advisers to help in the fight against the Taiping. An American adventurer, Frederick Townsend Ward, drilled a Chinese army in the use of modern firearms and Western tactics. After Ward's death, a British artillery officer, Charles "Chinese" Gordon (1833–1885), led the "Ever Victorious Army" in a campaign that destroyed the Taiping's reputation for invincibility. Shortly after Hong's death in the summer of 1864, government armies stormed Nanjing. An awed general reported to the emperor: "Not one of the 100,000 rebels . . . surrendered . . . but in many cases gathered together and burned themselves and passed away without repentance. Such a formidable band of rebels has been rarely known from ancient times to the present."

A TOTTERING DYNASTY

The Taiping rebellion cost an estimated 20 million lives and destroyed all but the last shreds of the Qing dynasty's mandate to rule. Even while Chinese armies were using Western aid to fight the Taiping, the Western powers were dispatching ships and soldiers to force new treaties on the dynasty. China's defeat by Britain and France in the brief Arrow War (1856–1858) led to the opening of eleven more treaty ports. When fighting flared again in 1859, British troops occupied Beijing, burning the glorious Imperial Palace in a wanton act of vandalism.

The dynasty tottered, too corrupt and too weak to govern effectively. The vast majority of Chinese lived in brutal poverty. With 90 percent of the land owned by rich landlords, the peasants worked at near-starvation wages. Some Christian missionaries tried to aid the poor, but most Westerners were too intent on making money to pay much attention to the great suffering of the Chinese people.

In 1861, the empress dowager Cixi (1835–1908) became China's ruler as regent for her son, the child-emperor Tongzhi. After his death in 1875, she continued as regent for the even younger emperor Guangxu (1871–1908). Intelligent, but unfamiliar with the ways of the wider world and under the influence of dishonest eunuchs, she ruled China like an empress of old. She spent extravagantly, once using funds intended for the modernization of the Chinese navy on a huge sculpted marble boat at the Summer Palace.

THE OVERSEAS CHINESE

Despite the terrible death toll brought by frequent famines and revolts, China's population continued to expand. By the 1870s, some 400 million Chinese were stretching the nation's resources to the limit. Millions fled the poverty and disorder in the countryside, only to find life equally hard in the teeming, filthy slums of China's cities. The government promoted a pioneer movement into China's sparsely settled west, but harsh natural conditions and the hostility of non-Chinese tribes limited internal expansion.

Millions of coastal Chinese took the difficult step of leaving their homeland. Boatloads of emigrants sailed from the ports of China. Many settled in Southeast Asia, where they took up traditional vocations such as farming, fishing, and shopkeeping. Some later became wealthy in business, mining, rubber planting, and shipping. Foreign contractors signed up armies of Chinese laborers for the even longer trip across the Pacific to the Americas. The passage was brutal, the laborers packed so tightly in the holds of the ships that they could hardly lie down. In Hawaii, South America, and the Caribbean islands, they were put to work in mines or on sugar plantations. Cheated of their pay, forced to work inhuman hours, and often whipped and chained, they became little more than slaves.

Large numbers of Chinese immigrants reached the West Coast of the United States near the end of the Cal-

A painting from about the fourteenth
century shows rice harvesters at work.
Since the dawn of agriculture nearly eight
thousand years ago, farming has been
a sacred calling for the Chinese.

The production of silk was an imperial monopoly and the process was a tightly held state secret. The many steps included bathing the silkworm eggs (left); unwinding the cocoons to produce silk thread (left, below); and weaving the silk thread into cloth (right, below).

A Ming dynasty painting depicts China's
three great spiritual teachers: (left to right)
Buddha, Confucius, and Laozi.

Brilliant and ruthless, Emperor Shi Huangdi unified China in 221 B.C., founding a centralized system of government that lasted into the twentieth century.

These terra-cotta warriors and warhorses are part of the army of life-sized figures from the tomb of Emperor Shi Huangdi.

Despite the extensive road network
built by the emperors, travel was often
arduous in China's vast interior.

Above: **A** mandarin official conducts
an inspection trip along the Great Wall,
China's immense but ineffective defense
against invaders from the north.

Despite the emperors' best efforts,
invaders, traders, and missionaries
penetrated China's defenses. Clockwise
from top left: Buddha, whose disciples
brought a new religion to China in the
first century A.D.; Jenghiz Khan, whose
Mongol warriors stormed into China
in 1210; a trading caravan from the
Middle East on the Silk Road.

A fifteenth-century painting shows a
Mongol chieftain hunting. Chinese artists
and civil servants served the Mongols,
eventually civilizing even the most
savage of China's conquerors.

Left: **K**ubilai Khan, last of the great Mongol rulers, adopted the dress and most of the customs of a Chinese emperor.

Below: **A** narrative painting (starting with the two figures at the upper left and proceeding clockwise) tells the story of Marco Polo's voyage from Venice to China, where he would serve for seventeen years as an imperial official for Kubilai Khan, before returning to Italy and reporting on his travels.

Above: A Manchu emperor is shown performing one of the endless series of rituals in the life of the "reigning son of Heaven."

Left, top: The Temple of Heaven, one of the world's architectural masterpieces, was built during the Ming dynasty as part of Beijing's Forbidden City.

Left: The peasant-born Zhu Yuanzhang founded the Ming dynasty and became one of China's most successful emperors.

Above: **A** painting from about the tenth century shows mandarin scholars studying the ancient Confucian texts that provided the basis for the civil service examinations.

Above: **A** bustling marketplace in ancient China. In the good times, the Chinese lived in a land of political and social stability unknown in the West.

Facing page, bottom: **U**pper-class women spent their lives in high-walled family compounds, their feet deformed by binding, and their minds and energies confined by the rigid customs of ancient Chinese society.

Above: **D**ynasties rose and fell, but
the mandarin civil service endured into
the twentieth century. The illustration
here shows the Beijing foreign office.

Right: **I**nside the Forbidden City,
a troupe of actors perform for
the imperial court.

Peasants climb a steep path beside
a cataract on the Yangzi in this
nineteenth-century engraving. While the
West entered the industrial age, China held
fast to its age-old methods and customs.

ifornia gold rush of 1848–1849. Too late to make their fortune in the gold fields, they worked abandoned claims and then drifted into other occupations as shopkeepers, laundry operators, and vegetable gardeners. Thousands signed on to build the first transcontinental railroads. By the 1880s nearly every city in North America had a Chinese community.

Chinese immigrants faced widespread hostility in a land where their customs, language, dress, and skin color differed greatly from those of the European-American majority. Chinese workers accepted low wages and long hours, angering American workers who were often in competition for the same jobs. Many Chinese immigrants expressed an ambition to return home once they had saved enough money to live comfortably in China—an attitude that offended many Americans. Inflamed by racist speakers and hate-filled newspapers, American workers attacked Chinese immigrants in a series of vicious riots.

In 1882, the United States Congress passed the Chinese Exclusion Act, which imposed a ban on the immigration of Chinese laborers, required all resident Chinese to carry registration certificates, and barred all Chinese from seeking American citizenship. Although some of the clauses were not enforced after the turn of the century, the Exclusion Act was not entirely abolished until 1946.

CALLS FOR REFORM

Even the emigration of millions could not ease the pressures building in China. A few brave scholars had been urging reform for a century and more, only to be ignored, banished, or executed. With the twentieth century approaching, a broader group of scholars called on the government to take radical action before it was too late. Students educated abroad and overseas Chinese added their voices to the calls for reform. They had seen the industrial might of the West, tasted the freedoms of democracy, and come to understand that China could not prosper without putting aside some of its ancient ways.

A powerful and upright Qing minister, Li Hongzhang (1823–1901), promoted a "self-strengthening" movement to import Western technology and methods, while preserving the best in traditional Chinese culture. He developed programs to send Chinese students to universities in Europe, the United States, and Japan; encouraged the building of railroads and modern factories; and engineered the construction of a small modern navy. Yet all of Li Hongzhang's diplomatic skill could not save China from the imperial designs of the Western powers. In the early 1880s, the French occupied northern Vietnam, ignoring Chinese claims to special privileges in the area. When negotiations broke down in 1884, the French fleet in the south China port of Fuzhou opened fire, destroying half of China's new "self-strengthening" fleet in an hour.

THE SINO-JAPANESE WAR

In 1894, the Qing received another brutal lesson in China's near helplessness against modern technology. Recently modernized Japan was the teacher. Japan had closed its ports to foreign traders in the 1630s and had refused to deal with the outside world for more than two centuries. But in 1853, an American naval squadron under Commodore Matthew Perry (1794–1858) sailed into Tokyo Bay to deliver a letter from the president of the United States suggesting the negotiation of a commercial treaty. The Japanese leaders were stunned by the size and firepower of the American warships. They recognized what the Chinese emperors had not: to compete with the industrialized West, they would have to modernize. In an amazing transformation, the Japanese changed their country from a medieval society into a modern state in a single generation. Confident and aggressive, Japan set out to dominate Asia.

Korea became Japan's first target. For centuries, Korean kings had paid homage to the Chinese emperors, accepting—often unwillingly—China's role as Korea's protector. When a rebellion broke out in the Korean capital of Seoul in the summer of 1894, China dispatched troops to protect the Korean royal family. But Japan, uninvited and unwanted, moved faster. Japanese armed forces occupied Seoul and ambushed unsuspecting Chinese troops en route to Korea. China tried to fight, but its forces were no match for the well-armed and well-trained Japanese. By the spring of 1895, China's fleet lay on the bottom of the ocean and its best troops were in headlong retreat toward Beijing. Forced to accept another humiliating peace treaty, China surrendered all influence over Korea, opened four more ports to foreign trade, paid a huge fine, and turned over the island province of Taiwan to Japan.

As China lay helpless, the great powers began slicing it into "spheres of influence," where they, not the Chinese government, ruled in all but name. Britain took the fertile Yangzi Valley. Russia controlled Manchuria and Mongolia. Germany, France, and Japan seized large coastal areas. Coming too late to the party, the United States in 1899 called for an "open door" policy that would preserve "the territorial and administrative integrity" of China, while granting all nations equal trading rights in the world's most populous nation. The other great powers refused to agree, but the Open Door Policy became the basis for America's foreign policy toward China and the eventual source of explosive friction with Japan.

THE HUNDRED DAYS REFORM

In the bitter aftermath of China's defeat by the Japanese, the calls for reform became a din. The reformers gained the ear of the young emperor Guangxu, urging him to free himself from the influence of his aging and conservative aunt, the empress dowager Cixi. While Cixi was absent from the capital in the summer of 1898, Guangxu began a startling series of reforms. For the next hundred days, a stream of decrees came from the palace. Henceforth, schools would teach both Chinese and Western subjects. The old civil service exams, based on the Confucian classics, would be radically updated. A restructured civil service would attract and promote people equipped with modern skills. The military would get the funds needed to become an effective fighting force. There would be a complete overhaul of the court system and the nation's often cruel and arbitrary laws. Police and prosecutors would root out corruption from the smallest village to the palace itself.

The reforms represented a direct assault on the power and privilege of Cixi's ruling elite. The enraged empress dowager returned to Beijing in September. Backed by powerful allies, she ordered Guangxu arrested and imprisoned on an island in the lake at the Summer Palace; executed many of his advisers; and withdrew nearly all the reform decrees. Within days, the promise of the reform movement lay in ruin. The dynasty returned to its corrupt and backward-looking ways.

THE BOXER REBELLION

As the new century opened, more and more Chinese focused their anger on the "foreign devils" carving up China "like a huge melon." Tens of thousands of Chinese joined the violently antiforeign Society of Righteous and Harmonious Fists. The Boxers, as they were called by Westerners, had no central leadership and no consistent program except to drive the "foreign devils" from China as a first step in restoring the Middle Kingdom to its ancient glory. In 1900, Boxer violence swept across northern China. The Boxers executed hundreds of missionaries and Western traders and thousands of their Chinese converts and employees. As a horde of Boxers streamed into Beijing, the Qing government abandoned its effort to put down the rebellion and began calling the rebels a loyal militia. The Boxers laid siege to Beijing's legation (foreign embassy) quarter for eight weeks, but they were too disorganized to overcome the small number of Western troops and armed civilians inside.

On August 14, 1900, some 20,000 Western troops marched into Beijing. The Boxers and the royal family fled the city. The Western powers took a terrible revenge. Western troops hunted down the Boxers—sometimes with the aid of missionaries—executing without trial even those only suspected of being sympathetic to the movement. Troops and civilians looted everything they could find of value and bragged about it in the newspapers. The Qing government was fined a crushing $333 million—nearly two times its annual budget—for its part in the uprising.

REFORM COMES TOO LATE

Allowed to keep her throne, Cixi reluctantly instituted some of the reforms that Guangxu had attempted. Both the emperor and Cixi died in the same month in 1908— she of old age, he allegedly of poison delivered at her order. One of Cixi's last acts was to promise the Chinese people a constitutional monarchy in which the emperor would be a figurehead and the power would rest with the people. But it was too late. Not even massive reform could save the system that had ruled China since the Qin dynasty over 2,000 years before.

6 Decades of Turmoil

In the first years of the twentieth century, tens of thousands of Chinese joined underground revolutionary organizations. Based in China's teeming cities, the revolutionary groups included students, professionals, soldiers, shopkeepers, industrial workers, and representatives of nearly every walk of life. All shared the common goal of destroying the doddering Qing dynasty and restoring China's independence from foreign domination. Some groups concentrated on spreading their vision of a better society through speeches and radical newspapers. Others went beyond words, as they tried to foment revolution through assassination and sabotage.

The fall of the last dynasty came with remarkable speed and little bloodshed by the standards of Chinese history. On October 9, 1911, an explosion ripped through a secret bomb factory in the city of Hankou in east central China. Qing police investigating the accident found documents listing the names of soldiers

70

who had enrolled in the revolutionary underground. Threatened with exposure and probable execution, soldiers in nearby Wuchang mutinied early the next morning. The mutiny spread rapidly, as garrisons in a dozen other cities announced that they would no longer take orders from the Qing government. Senior army officers refused to put down the mutiny, calling instead for massive reforms, including the formation of a national parliament and the election of a premier to govern the country.

In a desperate attempt to save the dynasty, the mother of the child emperor Puyi (1905–1967)—the son of the unfortunate Guangxu—agreed to surrender most of the dynasty's power to a premier: the reformist provincial governor Yuan Shikai (1859–1916). However, provincial assemblies meeting in Nanjing refused to accept a constitutional monarchy, declaring China a republic and electing Dr. Sun Yat-sen (1866–1925) president.

Dr. Sun was already a world-renowned figure. Educated in mission schools in Hawaii and a Western medical school in Hong Kong, he became a revolutionary activist in his twenties. In 1895, after a failed plot to overthrow the dynasty, he fled China, eventually settling in London. Qing agents tried to kidnap him, but he made a daring escape and recounted his dramatic story in Western newspapers. The resulting fame allowed him to travel widely, seeking support from overseas Chinese and sympathetic Westerners for a republican revolution in China. He developed a program of three principles for a new China: nationalism (the people should strive to build a strong China capable of managing its affairs without interference by other nations); democracy (government by the people through elected representatives); and "the people's livelihood" (the wealth of China should be managed for the good of all).

Dr. Sun accepted the presidency of the republic declared by the provincial assemblies. But to avoid civil war between his government in Nanjing and Yuan Shikai's in Beijing, he offered to resign in favor of Yuan if the Qing dynasty gave up its remaining power. Under pressure from Yuan and senior army officers, the royal family agreed to step down in exchange for an annual income and continued residence in Beijing's Forbidden City. On February 12, 1912, the little boy Puyi—the last emperor of China—abdicated and became a private, although very wealthy, citizen. Dr. Sun resigned, and Yuan Shikai became president.

THE REVOLUTION BETRAYED

China held its first national election in January 1913. Dr. Sun's Guomindang party (usually referred to by Westerners as the Nationalist party) won a large majority of seats in the new parliament. Unfortunately for China, President Yuan Shikai had little real sympathy for democracy. When Guomindang delegates harshly criticized his handling of the nation's finances, he fired all pro-Guomindang military governors and sent troops to destroy Guomindang strongholds. With the Guomindang driven underground, Dr. Sun fled to Japan. The ambitious Yuan tried to found a new dynasty, but he lacked the money and military power to impose his will on a China sick of emperors.

In 1914, World War I tore Europe apart. While the Europeans concentrated on killing one another in incredible numbers and the United States tried to avoid foreign involvements, Japan moved swiftly to fill the power void in China. Japan seized Germany's sphere of influence on China's northern coast and delivered a long list of demands to Yuan Shikai. The Japanese wanted extraordinary privileges in China, including the right to oversee the workings of the Chinese government and police force. Although Yuan had courted the support of the Japanese in founding his new dynasty, they were demanding too much in return. He sought Western support in refusing Japan's Twenty-one Demands, but the European powers were too busy and the United States put no teeth behind its objection. Threatened by Japan's modern army and navy, Yuan gave in to most of the demands.

Yuan Shikai died in 1916, his dreams of a new dynasty in tatters. The central government in Beijing became a shaky coalition of military leaders. Some were educated and patriotic, others mere bandits in military uniforms. Each warlord ruled his own region, often fighting his neighbors. As always in times of political division, the common people suffered greatly. Dr. Sun Yat-sen returned to China to begin the long task of rebuilding his Guomindang movement. Meanwhile, the war in Europe raged, chewing up an entire generation of young men. On the urging of Britain, France, Japan, and particularly President Woodrow Wilson (1856–1924) of the United States, the Beijing government declared war on Germany. Some 100,000 Chinese laborers traveled halfway around the globe to unload ships, build barracks, and dig trenches for the Allies.

THE MAY FOURTH MOVEMENT

When Germany surrendered in 1918, China expected recognition of its contribution to the Allied victory. But the Treaty of Versailles in 1919 gave the German concession area in Shandong province to Japan rather than returning it to the control of the Beijing government. The Chinese were appalled. On May 4, 1919, thousands of Chinese students gathered in Tiananmen Square at the center of Beijing to denounce the treaty and several cabinet ministers suspected of conspiring with the Japanese. Marching on the Japanese embassy, the students collided with club-swinging police who killed one student and left scores injured. News of the clash sparked sympathy strikes and demonstrations across China. The protests gave birth to the May Fourth Movement, an attempt to redefine Chinese culture to fit the modern world and to unite the people against the evils of warlordism, the landlord system, and foreign imperialism.

As the forces of revolution gathered again, a drought devastated central China. Forced to pay outrageous rents, the peasant farmers had little cash or food in reserve. Between 1919 and 1921, 500,000 people died of starvation and 20 million—40 percent of the area's estimated population—were left destitute. Conditions in many of China's crowded cities were barely better. Once again the cry went up across China for a strong, united, and just central government that could respond to the people's needs.

THE DREAM OF COMMUNISM

Bitterly disappointed by the Treaty of Versailles, some young Chinese rejected the Western democratic model. For them, the radical philosophy of communism seemed to offer a shining hope for China.

The idea of communism is very old: private ownership of property is destructive to social harmony. Throughout history, many thinkers have concluded that greed for money and possessions always creates a society of haves and have-nots. Some theorized that a better society could be built if property was held in common. All members of society would labor for the common good, receiving the necessities of life according to their needs. In the history of both East and West, there were numerous attempts to put communism into practice. Religious orders, utopian societies, and revolutionary groups—among them the Taiping—tried again and again. Bickering within destroyed most of the experiments, while the more threatening were suppressed, often with great bloodshed, by hostile churches or governments.

The German philosopher Karl Marx (1818–1883) laid out the framework of modern "scientific" communism. Marx stated that history could be explained as a conflict between the upper classes who owned the "means of production" and the working classes who provided the labor but received only a tiny percentage of the profits in wages. Marx believed that the world's workers (the proletariat) would eventually rise up to seize the means of production. During a period of state socialism directed by a "dictatorship of the proletariat," a harmonious, classless society would evolve to make government unnecessary, thus allowing the state to "wither away."

THE RUSSIAN REVOLUTION

Marx's theories attracted a small but dedicated following in Europe and America. In 1903, the revolutionary V. I. Lenin (1870–1924) helped found a Russian Communist party, the Bolshevik, to overthrow the Russian emperors, the czars. Frightful losses in World War I made Russia ripe for revolution. In February 1917, a spontaneous uprising by war-weary workers in the capital of Saint Petersburg overthrew the czarist government. Czar Nicholas II abdicated, and Russia's legislature, the Duma, elected a government of moderate reformers. Denied a role in the new government, the Bolsheviks plotted its downfall. The reform government squandered its meager public support by continuing the war against Germany, and the Bolsheviks staged a successful coup in November 1917. Lenin immediately pulled Russia out of the war and announced the formation of a Communist state. Russia and the subject nations that had been part of the czarist empire became the Union of Soviet Socialist Republics (USSR).

The USSR won many Chinese friends in July 1919, when it announced that it would return the Russian sphere of influence in Mongolia and northern Manchuria to Chinese control. Chinese radicals sought Soviet help in forming a Communist party in China. As the main sponsor of the international Communist organization, the Comintern, the Soviets were eager to help. Comintern agents traveled to China, where they conducted classes in Marxist-Leninist theory and the practical methods of revolutionary organization.

The Comintern agents selected able and dedicated Chinese students for advanced training in the USSR, France, and Japan. Among those who traveled to Paris in 1920 was a gifted young man named Zhou Enlai (1898–1976). The son of a prominent mandarin family, Zhou had received an excellent education, spoke several languages, and—even at the age of twenty-one— had the courtly manners of a diplomat. In a different century, he might have followed the traditional mandarin path through the examination system to a position of power at the imperial court. But the times made him a radical, and he had already served time in jail for helping to organize the May Fourth demonstrations.

Zhou's name would be linked in the decades to come with that of another young revolutionary: Mao Zedong (1893–1976). Mao came from a very different background. The son of a moderately well-off farming family from Hunan province, Mao had received a classical education as a child. While serving briefly as a soldier in the 1911 revolution against the Qing dynasty, he was deeply moved by the poverty and suffering he saw in rural China. He rejected life on the family farm and a marriage contract arranged by his parents in favor of a life of political activism. He moved to the city of Changsha, where he read widely in the political philosophy of East and West. In 1917, he began publishing a series of articles on the importance of physical exercise, equality for women, and the solidarity of the people in the revolutionary struggle against warlordism, imperialism, and the class system.

By 1921, Mao had become a leading organizer of radical activity in Hunan province. That July, he traveled to Shanghai to meet with a handful of like-minded radicals. Meeting in secret, they formed the Chinese Communist Party (CCP). Zhou Enlai was still in France, but he would join the CCP soon after his return to China. Other Communists with longer experience in revolutionary activity took the leading roles in the early years, but Mao and Zhou would eventually become the principal shapers of Chinese communism.

THE GUOMINDANG AND THE CCP

Dr. Sun Yat-sen's Guomindang party and the CCP shared the common goals of national reunification and an end to foreign imperialism. However, Dr. Sun opposed other aspects of communism, particularly the rigid state socialism of the Soviet model that did away with private enterprise and threatened personal initiative. At first, Dr. Sun refused to allow Communists to join the Guomindang. But in 1922, Lenin began loosening the grip of the state over economic activity in the USSR. Lenin's New Economic Policy (NEP) persuaded Dr. Sun that he might be able to work with the Communists after all. He accepted Soviet aid and promised to admit individual Communists to the Guomindang if the CCP gave up its faith in the Soviet model and disbanded its formal structure.

Concerned about the growing influence of Japan in the Far East, Soviet advisers pressured the Chinese Communists into a public acceptance of Dr. Sun's conditions. But rather than disbanding, the CCP became an underground organization, recruiting converts and preparing for the time when a Guomindang victory would unify the nation and end the interference of foreign powers in China's affairs. Then the CCP could emerge to make its bid for supreme power.

THE NATIONALIST REVOLUTION

In February 1923, Dr. Sun established a Nationalist government in Canton. The Soviet Union poured money into the creation of a well-armed and well-trained Nationalist army. A Soviet adviser, Mikhail Borodin, helped the Nationalists establish a military academy on Whampoa Island, downriver from Canton. Borodin skillfully balanced Guomindang and CCP influence at the academy. The first commandant was Chiang Kai-shek (1887–1975), a military adviser to Dr. Sun, while the political director was an ardent CCP member, the charming and sophisticated Zhou Enlai. Within a year, the academy produced the first crop of tough young officers to lead the Nationalist armies to victory.

Dr. Sun died on March 12, 1925, and Chiang Kai-shek became the dominant member of the Nationalist leadership. His army had already won its first victories against the southern warlords, and Chiang judged that conditions would soon be right for an all-out campaign to unify China. China seethed with rage against the corruption of the warlords and the outrages of the foreigners. Mao Zedong and hundreds of other Communist organizers were at work fomenting discontent among rural peasants and city workers. The Communist organizers set up people's governments, called soviets.

The soviets attacked social problems such as crime, drug addiction, prostitution, and the selling of children in hard times. In the countryside, peasant soviets confiscated land from the rich and redistributed it among poor farmers. In the cities, workers' soviets organized strikes and demonstrations against Chinese and foreign companies guilty of exploiting the labor of their Chinese workers. Local authorities, both Chinese and Western, struck back hard. In Canton and Shanghai, British troops fired on demonstrators, killing dozens.

In July 1926, Chiang set his military campaign in motion. Three Nationalist armies pushed steadily through southern China toward the Yangzi. Ahead of the armies, Communist agents organized local uprisings. Westerners fled in droves, often under protective fire from Western warships. Some warlords joined Chiang's advancing armies; others were crushed in heavy fighting. By early 1927, the Nationalist armies had captured all of southeastern China and were advancing on China's largest city, the great port of Shanghai.

While the army won victory after victory, there was bitter infighting between the conservative Chiang and more radical Guomindang and Communist leaders. Chiang made Nanchang his military base, while the radicals set up a national government in Wuhan. The Communists took a leading role in the Wuhan government, pushing for drastic economic and political reforms in the territory won by the Nationalist armies. The activities of the Communists threatened Chiang's domination of the Nationalist cause and put at risk the welfare of many of his influential and wealthy supporters. Chiang began plotting the destruction of the Communists and the Guomindang radicals.

In March 1927, as Chiang's troops surrounded Shanghai, Zhou Enlai led an uprising that established a Communist government in the city. Chiang was furious; the Communists were out of control. He met secretly with leaders of the underground Green Gang, headquartered in the city's French concession area. On April 12, with the support of Western authorities, the Green Gang attacked the Communists. Chiang's troops joined in the slaughter. Only a small percentage of the Communists, including Zhou, managed to escape into the countryside.

Chiang established a government in Nanjing and demanded that the Wuhan government disband. In the countryside, his troops killed thousands of peasants who had joined the Communist-organized soviets. Communist revolts in Nanchang and Canton were suppressed with incredible brutality. The surviving Communists went into hiding, their Soviet advisers fled China, and the Wuhan government collapsed. His position as undisputed leader of the government assured, Chiang began planning the conquest of China north of the Yangzi.

THE JIGSAW NORTH

Since the death of Yuan Shikai in 1915, northern China had been divided among rival warlords. Chiang expected most of them to cooperate with the Nationalists once his armies crossed the Yangzi. However, the wily Manchurian warlord Zhang Zuolin (1875–1928), who had occupied Beijing in late 1924, promised to be a major obstacle in the way of a Nationalist victory. Chiang's second great concern was a Japanese army protecting the foreign concession areas in the port of Tianjin and the Yellow River city of Jinan. A third threat lay farther north in the form of the Japanese Kwantung army protecting Japan's sphere of influence in Manchuria, China's vast northeastern province.

If anything, Zhang Zuolin faced an even more difficult situation than Chiang did. With the Communists on the run, Chiang had the temporary luxury of a secure home base. Zhang Zuolin, however, had to worry about the restless Kwantung army. Zhang Zuolin hated the Japanese, but lacked the military force to drive the Kwantung army out of Manchuria. The Kwantung officers, who despised Zhang Zuolin, wanted to attack the warlord and take control of Manchuria, but Japan's civilian government opposed any action that might draw criticism from the Western powers and cause trouble with the Soviet Union's forces along Manchuria's northern border.

The confused situation in Manchuria had been decades in the making. Members of Japan's ancient and powerful military class had coveted China's resources since Japan's rapid modernization in the late nineteenth century. In the Sino-Japanese War of 1894–1895, Japan's forces had taken control of Korea, long a dependency of China. A decade later, Japan had dealt the Russians a stunning defeat in the Russo-Japanese War to establish a sphere of influence in the southern half of Manchuria. Resource-poor Japan poured huge sums into the development of mines, factories, and railroads in Manchuria. To protect these investments, the Japanese government established the Kwantung army of tough Mongolian mercenaries and well-trained Japanese soldiers. Most of the Kwantung army's Japanese officers were aggressive militarists who dreamed of a great campaign to bring all of China—and eventually all of eastern Asia—under the domination of Japan.

Militarists controlled the Japanese government through World War I. With the Western powers distracted by the war in Europe, Japan brought heavy diplomatic and military pressure to bear against China with the Twenty-one Demands. Following World War I, however, the Western powers again took an interest in China, and Japan had to assume a less aggressive stance. Gradually, liberal democratic parties opposed to the militarists gained the upper hand in Japan's government, but the Kwantung army remained a stronghold of militarist sentiment. As Chiang began his march north in early 1928, officers in the Kwantung army devised a plot that they hoped would free them of both Zhang Zuolin and the pesky liberals at home.

THE NATIONALIST OFFENSIVE

Late in the winter of 1928, Chiang crossed the Yangzi and marched on Beijing. Sensing the growing power of the Nationalists, several of the remaining warlords came over to Chiang's side and most of the foreign powers extended grudging recognition to the Nationalist government. As the army neared the Yellow River, Chiang asked the Japanese to withdraw their troops from the river city of Jinan. At first it appeared that they would, but on May 3, a skirmish between the two armies turned into a pitched battle. Driven back from the city, Chiang rerouted his march and pushed on toward Beijing.

With the Nationalist armies descending on Beijing, Zhang Zuolin looked for an escape. The Japanese assured him that they would keep the Nationalists from advancing beyond the Great Wall if he would abandon Beijing and return to Manchuria. Zhang Zuolin agreed and loaded his staff aboard a train bound for the Manchurian capital of Mukden. A few miles short of Mukden, bombs exploded under the train, killing the warlord and many in his party.

The bombs had been placed by the plotters in the Kwantung army. They expected that the death of Zhang Zuolin would create a crisis in the Japanese government. Panicked by the threat of the Nationalists to the south and the Soviets to the north, the government's civilian ministers would place the armed services on a wartime footing for the defense of Japan's vital sphere of influence. The mobilization of the armed services would put militarists in position to sweep the civilian ministers aside and to order the complete occupation of Manchuria. If Chiang advanced north of the Great Wall, so much the better; the Japanese army would crush him and seize all of northern China.

The dreams of the Kwantung officers failed to materialize. Resolute liberals in the Japanese government refused to be stampeded into a mobilization, and Chiang skillfully ducked a confrontation. With the support of both the Nationalist and Japanese governments, Zhang Zuolin's son, Zhang Xueliang (1898–) took command of his father's army. The "Young Marshal," as Zhang Xueliang became known, proved a surprisingly competent successor to his father, despite a reputation as a playboy and a drug addict. He assured the

Japanese government of continued privileges in Manchuria, while at the same time pledging loyalty to Chiang and accepting a seat in the Nationalist State Council. A brooding Kwantung army, left with no one to fight, went back to protecting Japanese-owned railroads and mines. The Young Marshal raised the Nationalist flag over Mukden. For the first time since the fall of the Qing dynasty, China was united.

Much of the outside world applauded the Nationalist victory, but the new government brought little relief to the majority of China's common people, who continued to live in terrible rural poverty. Chiang ruled as a dictator over an almost unbelievably corrupt government. New warlords controlled half the country, sometimes collecting taxes fifty years in advance. Landlords bought up more land, making the life of the peasants even harder. Between 1928 and 1930, 5 million people starved to death and 400,000 peasants sold themselves or their children into servitude.

THE COMMUNISTS REBUILD

Badly wounded in Chiang's 1927 purge, the Communist party rebuilt in the mountains of Jiangxi province in southeastern China. Many of its early leaders were dead, and Mao Zedong and Zhou Enlai rose to senior positions in the reconstructed party.

Mao rethought the CCP's plans for revolution. In Russia, Lenin and his followers had organized city workers and managed to grab power with only a tiny minority of the country's population. But Chiang's army had crushed the workers' soviets in China's cities with little difficulty. For a Communist revolution to succeed in China, Mao concluded, the CCP would have to mobilize the great mass of peasants. After a long and heated debate, the leadership agreed. The CCP turned to strengthening the rural soviets that had survived Chiang's purge. The CCP issued strict rules for its political organizers and the soldiers of its Red Army. There would be no looting, no raping, no abuse of the peasants. Troops would pay for what they ate. All would treat the peasants with respect.

Alarmed at the CCP's renewed activity, Chiang added troops to his ongoing campaign against the Communists. In the immensity of rural China, it was a difficult task, but Chiang's troops made steady progress in snuffing out the rural soviets.

THE JAPANESE MILITARISTS STRIKE

Japanese militarists had not given up their ambitions after the failed plot in Manchuria in 1928. On September 18, 1931, Kwantung army officers set off bombs along the railway line outside the Manchurian capital of Mukden. They blamed the blasts on some of Zhang Xueliang's troops in the area and used the lie as an excuse to seize Mukden. Crack Japanese divisions poured in from nearby Korea, inflicting heavy losses on the Young Marshal's unprepared army. In Japan, senior army and navy officers demanded the government's full support. Cowed by the militarists, the civilian ministers accepted a conflict that they had tried to prevent.

Chiang Kai-shek was desperate to avoid war with Japan. He ordered Zhang Xueliang to retreat south of the Great Wall. By year's end, the Japanese occupied all of Manchuria. They installed Puyi, the last Chinese emperor and now a young man in his twenties, as the puppet ruler of a new state they named Manchukuo.

The Western powers objected to Japan's aggression but did nothing meaningful to force a Japanese withdrawal. Several factors contributed to the West's declining interest in China. The West's industrialized nations had severe problems at home as the world's economy staggered through the Great Depression, the decade of hard times that had begun in 1929. The European nations had never recovered from World War I and no longer had the power or the will to oppose

Japanese expansion. The United States had adopted a policy of "isolationism," avoiding foreign involvement wherever possible. America's refusal to join the League of Nations, the international peacekeeping organization established after World War I, left the League powerless to intervene in China.

After a few feeble protests, the West turned to other problems, leaving the Japanese militarists to make plans for conquering a gigantic empire that they politely called the "Greater East Asian Co-Prosperity Sphere." Hardly pausing after its conquest of Manchuria, the Kwantung army struck south toward Beijing. In China's coastal cities, there were boycotts and strikes against Japanese businesses. Japanese marines "protecting" the foreign concession area in Shanghai clashed with Nationalist troops, setting off a ferocious three-month-long battle in China's largest city. By the spring of 1933, Japanese troops held large sections of Shanghai, while far to the north, Japan's Manchurian army stood poised for an attack on Beijing and the important ports of Tianjin and Tanggu. Chiang had no choice but to accept a truce worked out by Western diplomats that left Shanghai neutralized and all of China north and east of the Great Wall under Japanese domination.

THE LONG MARCH

Instead of rallying the nation to resist further Japanese aggression, Chiang persisted in viewing the Communist "bandits" as the greatest threat to China's future. He shifted his best troops to the south and mounted an enormous campaign to destroy the Communist headquarters in Jiangxi province. His air force bombed the Jiangxi soviet day after day, while his army constructed a gigantic ring of roads and blockhouses around the Communists' mountain stronghold. By the fall of 1934, the pressure had become too much for the Communists. The leadership took a desperate gamble. On the night of October 16, the Red Army, led by Marshal Zhu De (1886–1976), broke through the ring of surrounding Nationalist armies and retreated westward in what would become known as the Long March.

The Long March is one of the incredible feats in military history. The Red Army suffered hardships beyond description. Under almost daily attack by Nationalist troops and planes, the Red Army crossed twenty-four rivers and hundreds of streams; eighteen mountain ranges, some as high as 16,000 feet (4,875 m); and great swamps where a misstep meant death in the sucking ooze. Often shoeless, canteens and knapsacks empty, the soldiers trudged on, covering mile after mile on their march into the safety of China's vast west and a place in the annals of human courage. In October 1935, after 6,000 miles (9,660 km) and 370 days on the march, the Red Army set up a new base at Yan'an in remote northern Shaanxi province. Some 80,000 of the original 100,000 soldiers had died on the Long March, but the Red Army had survived. Its example of discipline and dedication awed China and won millions of converts to communism.

The Long March brought Mao to the forefront of the Communist leadership. His brilliant theories of peasant revolution, his iron will, and his unshakable confidence in the face of disaster made him the dominant member of the leadership circle, with Zhu De and Zhou Enlai his principal allies.

DEMANDS FOR RESISTANCE

Chiang's policy of attacking the Communists while allowing the Japanese almost a free hand in north China aroused storms of protest. On December 9, 1935, thousands of anti-Japanese students rallied in Tiananmen Square in Beijing. Club-swinging police broke up the demonstration, but the protests spread across China. Nationalist generals demanded the right to fight the invaders. The Communists signaled that they would co-operate in a war against the Japanese. But Chiang remained firm in his policy of fighting the Communists first.

Zhang Xueliang, the Young Marshal, was among those who disagreed with Chiang's policy. Ordered by Chiang to abandon Manchuria, Zhang had retreated south of the Great Wall to a new base at Xi'an in Shaanxi province. Convinced that Japan was intent on conquering all of China, Zhang favored uniting forces with the Communists. In October 1936, Japanese troops attacked northwest of Beijing, meeting heroic Chinese opposition. A new wave of demonstrations swept China as the people demanded a united front to resist Japanese aggression.

On December 11, Zhang Xueliang met with his senior officers to set a desperate plan in motion. The next morning, units of Zhang's army stormed Chiang's headquarters outside Xi'an, killing his bodyguards and taking the "generalissimo" captive. Three weeks of complicated negotiations followed as Zhang tried to nail together an anti-Japanese united front. Zhou Enlai flew to Xi'an on December 16 to convince Zhang that only Chiang Kai-shek had the power and prestige to lead the front. Zhang asked Chiang, but Chiang refused to accept leadership until he was released and flown to safety in Nanjing.

To guarantee Chiang Kai-shek's safe passage, Zhang volunteered to accompany him on the flight to the Nationalists' southern capital. It was an act of remarkable courage, since Zhang knew that he would be at Chiang's mercy once the plane landed. In Nanjing, Zhang was court-martialed and sentenced to ten years in prison. Chiang commuted the prison sentence to house arrest, but extended the term indefinitely. In 1993, the aged Zhang was still officially under arrest in Taiwan.

JAPAN INVADES

Chiang had little enthusiasm for a united front, but he could no longer ignore the calls for alliance with the Communists. Grudgingly, he agreed. The united front was soon put to the test. In the summer of 1937, the Japanese launched an all-out invasion of China. Chinese soldiers fought with astonishing courage, losing 250,000 men killed and wounded in the fight for Shanghai alone, but the Japanese military machine was too powerful to defeat. Chiang moved his capital to Hankou, leaving orders for the defense of Nanjing to the last man. But his general fled, and Japanese troops ravaged the city in an orgy of rape, torture, and murder that stunned the world. An estimated 150,000 civilians and captured soldiers died in the infamous "Rape of Nanjing."

The Japanese army plowed westward in the spring of 1938. In an act of desperation, Chiang's engineers blew up the Yellow River dikes. The floodwaters stalled the Japanese advance for three months, but at the cost of 11 cities, 4,000 villages, and hundreds of thousands of Chinese lives. In the fall of 1938, Chiang abandoned Hankou, retreating to remote Chongqing, far up the Yangzi. Millions of Chinese civilians followed the retreat into the forbidding west to join the Communist or Nationalist armies. In countless long marches, they carried anything that might be used to fight the Japanese. Workers lugged factory machinery, students the equipment from university laboratories, and shopkeepers their wares.

The immensity of China eventually slowed the invaders. Holding out in Chongqing, Chiang began to receive military aid from the West. But rather than go on the offensive against the Japanese, Chiang hoarded his new equipment for a renewed campaign against the Communists. The Communists were again showing themselves masters of peasant organization as they built guerrilla armies to make hit-and-run attacks on the Japanese across northern and eastern China. Frightened by the growing Communist influence, Chiang ordered the Red Army out of what he claimed as Nationalist territory. In January 1941, Nationalist forces ambushed the Communist New Fourth Army in Jiangxi province, sparking a major battle. After that, Communist and Nationalist forces fought each other almost as often as they fought the Japanese.

The United States declared war on Japan the day after Japanese carrier aircraft struck the United States naval base at Pearl Harbor, Hawaii, on December 7, 1941. While Chinese forces held down two-fifths of the Japanese army, the United States started the slow process of gaining the offensive against the Japanese empire. President Franklin D. Roosevelt (1882–1945) dispatched General Joseph "Vinegar Joe" Stilwell (1883–1946) to coordinate operations with Chiang. Stilwell was appalled by the massive corruption and waste in the Nationalist army. He demanded a reorganization of the Nationalist war effort and a genuine attempt at cooperation with the Communists. Chiang refused and complained to Washington about Stilwell's arrogance.

After a long contest of wills with Chiang, Stilwell was replaced by a general more sympathetic to Chiang. Many of the American military and political experts— including those who had visited Yan'an and gained considerable respect for the Communists—were recalled from China. Meanwhile, Chiang and his American-educated wife were portrayed as heroic figures by the Western press. Madame Chiang addressed the United States Congress and delivered speeches across the country, painting a glowing picture of the heroism, popularity, and good works of the Nationalists. State Department experts who cautioned that the true picture was not that rosy found themselves transferred to other assignments. In a decision that would cost the United States dearly, the Roosevelt administration put all its hopes in the Nationalists.

World War II ended in August 1945, after the United States dropped two atomic bombs on Japan. Japanese forces in China began a headlong retreat, leaving chaos and devastation behind.

THE COMMUNIST REVOLUTION

Within days of the Japanese surrender, civil war raged in China. Soviet troops seized Manchuria and turned over vast stockpiles of Japanese weapons to Communist guerrillas and regular troops. The United States airlifted Nationalist soldiers to key cities surrendered by the Japanese, at the same time trying to arrange a reconciliation between the Nationalists and the Communists. It was hopeless; too many years of bitterness and treachery separated the two sides.

Chiang had lost much of his prestige at home and abroad. The Chinese people, angered by the brutality, corruption, and inefficiency of the Nationalist government, sided more and more with the Communists. Nationalist troops looted everywhere they went, while the Red Army held to its strict rules of proper conduct. The economy lay in ruins. Runaway inflation robbed the nation's currency of so much of its value that it literally took an armload of money to buy the simplest necessity. Flooding in the south destroyed the rice crop, creating famine all over China. Yet the Nationalists seemed neither willing nor able to do anything to help. For millions of Chinese fighting to survive in a class structure generations old, Mao's policies of seizing the land and wealth of the rich and giving them to the poor seemed to promise a better tomorrow.

After two years of bloody guerrilla warfare against the Nationalists, Mao announced that the Red Army was ready to fight Chiang's forces head on. In the early fall of 1948, a brilliant young general, Lin Biao (1908–1971), smashed the Nationalist armies in southern Manchuria. Some 400,000 of Chiang's best troops surrendered or deserted. The Red Army's commander in chief, Marshal Zhu De, ordered Lin Biao to attack the city of Xuzhou, on the main railroad line connecting Shanghai and Nanjing with the interior. Lin Biao's 600,000 soldiers were supported in the battle against an equal number of Chiang's troops by two million peasant laborers organized by Deng Xiaoping (1904–), a senior party official of great talent. After a 65-day pounding, the Nationalist army disintegrated. Lin Biao turned north, capturing Tianjin and receiving the surrender of Beijing on January 31, 1949.

In the spring and summer of 1949, the Communist armies drove south, routing every Nationalist force in their way. Chiang retreated to the island of Taiwan off the southeast coast, where he would survive under the protection of the United States. On the mainland, the Communists celebrated their victory by proclaiming the People's Republic of China on October 1, 1949.

7 The Building of the People's Republic

Huge problems faced the new leaders of China in 1949. For over a century, China had known nearly continuous war and turmoil. The nation had little modern industry, there was terrible poverty in most parts of the country, and much of the outside world was hostile.

As chairman of the Chinese Communist Party (CCP), Mao was the most powerful leader in China. He directed a sweeping series of reforms. The government fixed prices and rationed food and other necessities; took over most large businesses and factories; confiscated the land of the rich landlords and began dividing it among the peasants; stockpiled grain in case of famine; expanded education and medical care; began a massive public-works campaign; granted equal rights to women; passed child-labor laws; and instituted a campaign against corruption, opium smoking, and prostitution.

A CONTINUING REVOLUTION

"Revolution," Mao wrote, "is not a dinner party," and the destruction of the class system caused incalculable suffering. Exploited for countless generations, the peasants vented their rage by executing over a million landlords without trial. Communist officials—called cadres—organized mass meetings of angry workers and peasants to try "reactionaries" who had opposed the revolution. These people's courts ordered the execution of hundreds of thousands and sent millions more to labor camps for "reeducation." (Among those "reeducated" was the last emperor, Puyi, who was captured by Soviet troops at the end of World War II and turned over to Communist authorities. Released in 1959, he spent the remaining eight years of his life—apparently quite happily—as a gardener.)

The CCP denounced Confucianism, the philosophy that had been used to justify the old class system. Churches and temples were closed or put under tight government control. Communism and "Mao Zedong thought" took the place of the old philosophies and religions of China. The leadership began a vigorous campaign to spread the ideology of communism. Schools gave top priority to the teachings of Marx, Lenin, and Mao. Cadres organized mass meetings to educate adults in communism. Newspapers and radio stations became government propaganda organs. The government banned or heavily censored most Western books, movies, and plays, while directing China's writers and moviemakers to concentrate on telling stories of the glorious revolutionary struggle.

Anyone who criticized communism or China's leadership risked harsh punishment. The CCP preached the need for "constant vigilance" to protect the revolution from its many enemies: the Nationalist government on Taiwan, the capitalist West, and particularly the old traditions of Chinese life. Under the guidance of the party, the people were to live each day with revolutionary discipline, forever guarding against the tendency to slip back into old ways. Individual liberties of speech, religion, and assembly were examples of "spiritual pollution" from the West and were to be rejected for the greater good of the revolution. Even makeup, colorful clothes, and elaborate hairstyles were labeled antirevolutionary displays of individuality by the party.

Yet the CCP had to rein in its revolutionary zeal when it came to rebuilding China's industries and running its large cities. The Guomindang purges of the 1920s and 1930s had largely destroyed the Communist party in the cities. Few of the rural leaders who had rebuilt the party and led it to victory in the revolution had the technical and managerial skills needed to deal with urban and industrial problems. Tens of thousands of China's best educated and most talented people had fled China as Chiang Kai-shek's government crumbled, and many who remained were unenthusiastic about the Communist takeover. With a shortage of trained experts in its ranks, the CCP was forced to keep many non-Communist managers, professionals, and technicians in their prerevolution jobs.

THE STRUCTURE OF THE NEW GOVERNMENT

The Communists established a complicated structure to govern the People's Republic of China (PRC). The CCP set all major policies, although to avoid the appearance of one-party rule, it allowed the continued existence of a few minor parties. The central government instituted and administered the CCP's policies. The People's Liberation Army (PLA) was assigned the job of protecting the PRC from enemies abroad and from disturbances within, while also contributing its vast human resources to large public-works projects and rural harvests.

The leadership of party, government, and army overlapped. Mao was chairman of the CCP, chairman of the CCP's Military Committee, and also chairman of the government's Central People's Governing Council—a combination that gave him policy control over all three power centers. Zhou Enlai's primary job was supervising the central government as premier of the PRC, but he was also foreign minister and had a prominent voice in developing army and CCP policies as a member of the five-person standing committee of the CCP's Politburo. Similarly, Zhu De was both commander of the Red Army and another member of the Politburo's standing committee. In all, about a dozen officials held similar multiple offices that gave them tremendous power. Although granted the vote by the Chinese constitution of 1949, the people had little real say in the governing of their country.

THE KOREAN WAR AND A HOSTILE WORLD

The Communist leaders had many reasons to fear for the future of the Chinese revolution. The brief alliance between the Western democracies and the Soviet Union had soured shortly after World War II, leaving the two sides locked in a cold war. The Nationalist defeat in China was considered a monumental disaster by many in the West. Western hard-liners, including some members of the United States Congress, talked of rebuilding the Nationalist armies on Taiwan to "retake China." More practical leaders spoke of "containing communism" within its existing borders.

Korea became the flash point. At the end of World War II, Soviet and American troops had occupied opposite ends of the Korean peninsula. Ignoring the newly formed United Nations' repeated requests for free elections, the Soviets set up a Communist government in the north. On June 25, 1950, Communist North Korea invaded republican South Korea. The United Nations approved a "police action" in support of the south. Sixteen nations contributed forces to an army commanded by General Douglas MacArthur (1880–

1964) of the United States Army. On September 15, with North Korean troops on the point of victory, MacArthur launched a daring amphibious landing at Inchon near the captured South Korean capital of Seoul. Within two months, the Communists were driven back into North Korea.

Meanwhile, President Harry S Truman (1884–1972) sent the United States Seventh Fleet to patrol the Taiwan Strait in case the Chinese Communists tried to invade Taiwan while the Western nations were occupied with the war in Korea. The PRC denounced the naval patrols and harshly criticized the UN as its troops pushed into North Korea in November 1950, seemingly intent on unifying Korea by force. Late in November, as UN troops reached the Yalu River separating Korea from China, the Chinese army struck from Manchuria in overwhelming force. Driven back into South Korea, the UN army rallied again. After more months of heavy fighting, the war settled into a bloody stalemate along the thirty-eighth parallel separating North Korea from South Korea.

Some two million soldiers were killed or wounded by the time an armistice was concluded in July 1953. The bloodshed destroyed any chance for friendly relations between the PRC and the United States, or a peaceful reunification of Taiwan and the mainland. The United States signed a mutual defense treaty with Taiwan and barred the PRC from admission to the UN. It would take nearly two decades for the PRC and the United States to take the first steps toward a reconciliation.

THE ELDER BROTHERS

In its isolation from the West, the PRC grew even closer to the Soviet Union. Through the early 1950s, China's leaders urged the people to learn from their "elder brothers"—the thousands of advisers sent by the USSR. The PRC patterned its economic, educational, military, and police systems on the Soviet model. The Communist leaders attacked Western influences in China, ending all foreign investment, confiscating most private businesses, and instituting central planning of the economy. Following the Soviet example, the central government issued five-year plans for modernizing the economy. The first five-year plan (1953–1957) produced a huge increase in industrial and raw materials production. The quality of life was raised for tens of millions of Chinese, as the government conducted campaigns to improve medical care, disease control, literacy, and sanitation.

However, the government failed miserably with a series of complicated agricultural reforms. After the revolution, farmers had received shares of the land once owned by rich landlords. Except for harvest and planting times when they worked together in "mutual aid teams," peasant families cultivated their small farms independently. Thanks to the peasants' skill, energy, and traditional love of the land, farm production and income rose sharply. Yet Mao saw private ownership of the land as a threat to his vision of a classless Communist society. Before long, he feared, the best and most fortunate of the small farmers would emerge as a new class of rural rich people. At Mao's urging, the CCP chose a new direction for agricultural development.

In 1952, the government started pressuring the peasants to form cooperative farms that could be worked by teams of peasants using modern methods. The cooperative-farm policy backfired. Peasants devoted their greatest energies to the small private plots they were allowed to keep, and overall agricultural production fell. Stubbornly holding to its policy, the government expanded the size and number of the cooperatives, but production continued to slide. Deeply frustrated, Mao drafted a new agricultural plan. The government would confiscate all private land and combine the cooperatives into huge collective farms, where armies of peasants would work directly under the direction of rural party cadres. The Soviet advisers objected, citing the dismal failure of collective farms in the USSR. But to the dismay of the advisers and the peasants, Mao rammed his plan through the leadership.

The cooperative farms had been a disappointment; the collective farms were a disaster. Cadres with no experience in farming ordered the wrong crops planted. Expensive machinery ground to a halt for lack of maintenance. Peasants, deprived of both land and any sense of independence, worked halfheartedly. Agricultural production plunged.

THE HUNDRED FLOWERS CAMPAIGN

The disaster split the Communist leadership. Opposing Mao were several senior officials, who became known as the pragmatists since they were more interested in practical solutions to the PRC's economic woes than in elaborate theories of continuing revolution. The pragmatists wanted to streamline the party and government bureaucracies for the efficient management of a planned series of reforms. Mao, however, saw the emergence of a class of cautious planners and managers as little more than a return to the mandarin system of old China. The policy debate within the party's inner circle became a power struggle as the pragmatists worked to undercut Mao. Mao fought back by calling for a national debate on China's future: "Let a hundred flowers bloom and a hundred thoughts contend."

By inviting the people to participate in the debate, Mao expected to prove that the future of communism in China depended not on bureaucratic efficiency but on the revolutionary enthusiasm of the masses. Instead, the Hundred Flowers Campaign revealed a massive distaste for communism as it was being practiced in the PRC. Between May 1 and June 7, 1957, there was a tremendous outpouring of anger. Students and intellectuals led attacks against the CCP, its leaders, and an assortment of government policies, particularly the forced collectivization of agriculture. At Beijing University, students plastered a wall with posters demanding individual freedoms and open elections. In some cities, the protests turned violent as people assaulted party cadres and the system they represented.

Aghast at what he had unleashed, Mao denounced the flowers as "poisonous weeds." On June 7, after five weeks of free debate unknown in China, the government smashed the movement. Tens of thousands of intellectuals were arrested, labeled "rightists," and sent to prisons or labor camps—some for as long as twenty years. Three student radicals were tried and shot in front of their fellow students. Once again, China lost many of its best educated and most talented people.

THE GREAT LEAP FORWARD

Mao refused to accept that the intellectuals and students spoke for the people. He implied that he had engineered the Hundred Flowers Campaign to smoke out the rightists thwarting the will of the masses. Marshaling a shaken CCP, he laid out an even more radical plan for continuing revolution: the Great Leap Forward.

In December 1958, the Central Committee of the CCP ordered the merging of the PRC's 740,000 cooperative and collective farms into 26,000 communes. Some 120 million rural households—a full 99 percent of the peasant population—would become cogs in the immense machinery of the commune system, in which all aspects of individual and family life would be directed by party cadres. Commune authorities would control the housing, education, medical care, work assignments, recreation, political expression, and even cooking and eating arrangements of commune members. Couples would have to ask permission to marry or to have a child. Mothers would leave their children in commune day-care facilities while they labored on the land or in one of the thousands of new rural factories. Gigantic armies of peasants would open vast new tracts of farmland, clear forests, and build dikes and roads.

The Great Leap Forward has no parallel in human history. Never before had there been an attempt to organize so many people so completely. Several factors made it possible: the Chinese Confucian tradition dictated an acceptance of authority; the suppression of the Hundred Flowers Campaign had silenced nearly all intellectual voices opposed to the CCP and its policies; and—perhaps most important of all—the Communists were ruthless in their indoctrination and organization of the masses. Anyone who questioned, dissented, lagged in obedience, or failed to display enthusiasm for communism and Mao Zedong thought risked immediate and harsh punishment.

The Great Leap Forward turned into a giant step backward for China. Commune authorities ignored centuries of peasant wisdom as they directed the planting of rice and wheat. The crops failed. When the government ordered a huge increase in steel production, unskilled cadres directed equally unskilled peasants in building a million crude blast furnaces. Peasants gathered every available ounce of scrap metal—some families even contributing their pots and pans—but the furnaces produced unusable slag. Dozens of similar efforts produced similarly shoddy results, while frightened cadres tried to hide their blunders with wildly inflated production figures. All the while, China wasted energy and resources at a spectacular rate. Entire forests disappeared under the ax, the wood burned as fuel in a country where good lumber was already scarce. Deforestation caused wind and water erosion that ruined thousands of acres of precious farmland.

Torrents of rain rushed unchecked down denuded hillsides, sending rivers boiling over dikes that had protected the land for centuries.

In 1959, Tibetans rebelled against Chinese occupation. The People's Liberation Army suppressed the uprising with a brutality that roused outrage around the world. That same year, the armies of China and previously friendly India clashed in the disputed borderlands between the two nations. Disgusted with Mao and the folly of the Great Leap Forward, the Soviet Union withdrew its advisers in 1960. The Communist superpowers denounced each other for "deviating" from true communism, opening a rift that would last for nearly three decades. After China tested its first nuclear bomb in 1960, the USSR began preparing for a possible war between the communist giants.

MAO'S POWER EBBS

The troubles abroad added to the deepening crisis in China, where the Great Leap Forward was becoming a disaster of incredible proportions. With grain reserves already low, the weather turned bad and the age-old curse of Chinese life struck: famine. Between 1959 and 1962, an estimated 20 million people—some within an hour's drive from Beijing—starved to death.

Mao largely saw what he wanted to see, but pragmatic party leaders confronted the disaster. In heated policy debates within the party's inner circle, the pragmatists argued against Mao's belief that the masses could modernize China with little more than willpower and revolutionary zeal. Premier Zhou Enlai; Liu Shaoqi, the president of the republic; and Deng Xiaoping, secretary-general of the CCP, argued that China must place its future in the hands of a new generation of dedicated scientists, technicians, economists, and managers.

Under pressure from the pragmatists, Mao "retired

from the front line" to write and to think. Although Mao could still exert great influence as chairman of the CCP, the pragmatists took over management of the economy and the direction of China's modernization. China rebounded from the disaster of the Great Leap Forward. By the mid-1960s, the pragmatists' emphasis on proven methods and careful central planning reversed the declining standard of living.

THE CULTURAL REVOLUTION

Mao watched with increasing frustration as the pragmatists altered his vision of a continuing revolution and a truly classless society. In 1966, he declared the Great Proletarian Cultural Revolution, enlisting an army of young people as Red Guards to overthrow the "revisionists" who were subverting the revolution.

For millions of Chinese, particularly the restless young, the charismatic Mao was still "the Great Helmsman"—the intrepid captain who had guided the revolution to victory against the Nationalists. If China had failed to achieve the great goals of those glorious days, it was only because traitors had wrested the wheel away from him. When Mao called on the Red Guards to "turn the guns on the revisionist headquarters," they responded with a vengeance.

The Red Guards accused hundreds of thousands of intellectuals and government officials of deviating from Mao Zedong thought. The accused were beaten, forced to confess to "counterrevolutionary crimes," marched through the streets wearing dunce caps and placards, and then imprisoned or sent to work in distant communes. Artists, scientists, college professors, doctors, and countless other well-educated people were soon cleaning latrines, slopping hogs, and planting rice. Liu Shaoqi died under house arrest in an isolated city. Deng Xiaoping was sent into rural exile. Only

Zhou Enlai had the power and the prestige to keep his position.

Over the next several years, the Red Guards persecuted perhaps 100 million people. Thousands were beaten to death, and thousands more committed suicide. Children denounced their parents as "capitalist roaders." Red Guards broke into homes in search of books, art, and letters that could be considered counterrevolutionary. In an orgy of destruction intended to rid China of the influence of the past, they burned priceless artworks and manuscripts, defaced ancient shrines, and tore down magnificent buildings dating from the old China. Lacking central leadership and beyond any restraint, Red Guard factions clashed in bloody street battles. Workers, tired of Red Guard bullying, fought for their factories and neighborhoods. Even Mao was frightened by the huge excesses of the Red Guards. Pressed by Zhou Enlai and others, he began to rein in the violence. The People's Liberation Army took to the streets to restore order.

THE LIN BIAO PLOT

The PRC's defense minister, General Lin Biao, had stood by Mao in the early 1960s when he was shunted aside by the pragmatists. Lin had compiled a book, *Quotations from Chairman Mao*, which reinforced Mao's stature as a great leader. In shortened form, it became the" Little Red Book" waved by hundreds of thousands of demonstrating Red Guards. For his stalwart backing, Mao chose Lin as his successor in 1969. Within a year, however, Mao began undermining the ambitious general he no longer trusted.

What exactly happened is still unclear. According to the party line, Lin Biao tried to save his political future by orchestrating the assassination of Mao. When his plot failed, Lin panicked. He fled by plane to the Soviet Union, but the plane crashed in Mongolia, killing all aboard. Across China, people listened in disbelief to the news that Lin Biao—so recently a hero second only to Mao—had been a traitor all along. Where were they to put their faith next?

8 New Hopes, Broken Hopes

The turmoil of the Cultural Revolution faded slowly. Disenchanted with Mao, more and more people looked to Premier Zhou Enlai as the symbol of law and stability in China. Zhou had worked diligently behind the scenes to contain the worst of the Cultural Revolution's excesses. He had protected the nuclear weapons and defense industries against the Red Guards, maintained critical government services, and tried to minimize the influence of Lin Biao and the military. Perhaps most important of all, he had protected several senior pragmatists—including China's future leader, Deng Xiaoping—during their rural exile.

In the early 1970s, Zhou Enlai began quietly arranging the "rehabilitation" and reappointment to high positions of Deng Xiaoping and other important pragmatists. The pragmatists had to move cautiously to avoid crossing Mao and the radicals who still held most of the power in the PRC. Grown old and in declining health, Mao was increasingly under the influence of his wife, Jiang Qing (1914–), a radical who wanted to continue the Cultural Revolution. Hidden from the eyes of the people and most of the rest of the world, a long, complicated struggle began for the future leadership of China.

OPENING TO THE WEST

Like Mao, Premier Zhou had grown old. In his last years he hoped to end China's long isolation from the outside world. He cooled the PRC's revolutionary propaganda and sent quiet assurances to the West that the PRC was interested in peaceful coexistence. Under pressure from nations that wanted China to rejoin the world community, the United States dropped its opposition to the PRC's membership in the United Nations. In October 1971, the PRC took China's seat among the five permanent members of the UN Security Council.

The change in United States policy made it possible for Zhou to open secret talks with Dr. Henry Kissinger (1923–), national security adviser to the president of the United States. Together they planned a dramatic event. In early 1972, to the astonishment of the world, President Richard M. Nixon (1913–) flew to China. A lifelong anticommunist, Nixon had a friendly meeting with Mao and was soon toasting Zhou at a banquet in Beijing's Great Hall of the People. A Great Wall of distrust between East and West had been breached at last.

THE DEATH OF ZHOU

An outpouring of grief followed the announcement of Premier Zhou Enlai's death on January 8, 1976. The people had come to view this quiet and wise man as the "elder brother" of all Chinese. At his funeral, Vice Premier Deng Xiaoping delivered a eulogy praising Zhou for his modesty and prudence—virtues rarely seen in Mao and the radicals. His words sounded, at least to some, like a challenge to the radicals. Deng Xiaoping became the target of a renewed campaign by the radicals to discredit the pragmatists.

On April 4, 1976, people all over China prepared for the annual Qingming festival honoring the spirits of ancestors. In Beijing's Tiananmen Square, a crowd of mourners placed wreaths, banners, and placards honoring Zhou on the memorial to the martyrs of the revolution. By the next morning, the police—apparently on the orders of Jiang Qing's radicals—had removed all the tributes. An angry crowd gathered to protest the insult to the memory of Premier Zhou. As the crowd swelled toward 100,000, fighting broke out with police. Demonstrators set police cars on fire and forced their way into government buildings. Most of the crowd went home in the early evening. A few hours later, security forces entered the square in force to arrest or disperse the remaining protesters.

Three days later, the Central Committee relieved Deng of all his posts. Exercising the virtue of prudence he had praised in Zhou, Deng retired to Canton where he could expect protection by the region's pragmatic military commander. While Jiang Qing's radicals and Deng's pragmatists maneuvered, an obscure politician emerged to become the likely successor to Mao. As a provincial party chairman, Hua Guofeng had courted Mao's favor. Mao responded by naming Hua head of the PRC's public security forces. Jiang Qing's radicals viewed him as a tool, but Hua kept his lines open to the pragmatists. Following Deng's disgrace, Hua was named premier and first vice chairman of the CCP, second only to Mao.

DEATH OF THE GREAT HELMSMAN

Mao Zedong, who had shaped the course of one of history's greatest revolutions, died shortly after midnight on September 9, 1976. The death of the Great Helmsman roused little of the sorrow that had followed the death of Zhou Enlai. For the Chinese people, Mao had become the object of awe and fear more than affection. Hua Guofeng became chairman of the CCP and—at least in title—the most powerful person in China. Less than a month later, Hua astonished everyone by ordering the arrest of Jiang Qing and three of her main radical allies. The government let loose a barrage blaming "the Gang of Four" for nearly everything wrong in China. They were tried in 1980, convicted of numerous crimes, and sent to prison for life.

Although Hua had managed to win the PRC's highest positions, he lacked the prestige and talent to hold on to power. Senior military officials demanded the "rehabilitation" of Deng Xiaoping. By July 1977, Deng was again holding a high post and exerting great influence in the government. He skillfully outmaneuvered Hua. By 1980, Hua had lost his major titles and was again an obscure member of the Central Committee.

SETTING A NEW COURSE

Much needed to be done to put China back on the path to modernization. Ten years of turmoil and mismanagement during the Cultural Revolution had badly damaged the economy, displaced many of the government's best officials, and nearly destroyed the educational system. Deng laid out a course for a very new direction.

During his long years in rural exile, Deng had reached some conclusions about Mao's brand of communism. One of the most important was that China must avoid another "cult of personality" like the one that had grown around Mao. Carefully, he set about cutting Mao's reputation down to size. The CCP's media began issuing a new propaganda line, explaining that Mao had fallen out of touch with the people in his old age and made errors under the influence of the Gang of Four. Although China would be forever grateful to Mao for his contributions to the revolution, it was time to move on. His many pictures disappeared from China's buildings, and references to Mao Zedong thought became scarce in the media.

Deng persuaded thousands of elderly party officials and army officers to retire so that younger people with progressive ideas could advance. He surrendered most of his own positions, nominating younger leaders for the top offices in the CCP and the government. He retained only the chairmanship of the Military Committee of the CCP, a position that would allow him behind-the-scenes influence.

THE FOUR MODERNIZATIONS

Deng and his fellow pragmatists called on the people to work for the Four Modernizations: an ambitious program to modernize national defense, science and technology, agriculture, and industry.

The People's Liberation Army, the world's largest army, had fallen behind the times in military technology and training. The PLA would buy new weapons and adopt tactics more suited to the demands of modern warfare.

Before the Cultural Revolution, Chinese scientists had made great strides in science and technology. China had exploded nuclear bombs and launched earth satellites. Under the Four Modernizations, the government would build new laboratories where scientists could work free of political interference.

During the Cultural Revolution, an entire generation had lost the chance for a meaningful education. Schools and universities closed for months and years at a time, while students were sent to the countryside to "learn from the peasants." Many skilled teachers— hated intellectuals—spent most of a decade in "reeducation" camps or menial jobs. The pragmatists "rehabilitated" the disgraced teachers and reopened schools.

Mao Zedong thought no longer dominated the curriculum, as students learned practical skills to help China modernize. Thousands of the best students received scholarships for advanced training abroad.

The pragmatists' plan for modernizing industry and agriculture departed radically from Mao's policies. Deng proposed a system of incentives and limited free enterprise to stimulate productivity and to raise China's standard of living. Under Deng's "responsibility system," factory work units would set their own work rules, production goals, and prices in competition with other factories. Profits—unacceptable in Mao's China—would mean higher wages for workers. Workers who showed special ability or effort would receive bonuses. Critical heavy industries (such as steel, energy, and chemicals) would remain under government control, but people could set up factories in nonessential industries in open competition with government factories producing similar goods.

In the countryside, peasants would no longer labor in large groups on the commune land under the direction of party cadres. Instead, each family or small groups of families could sign a 15-year lease to farm commune land. Part of the crop would go to the government, while the peasants could sell the rest in a free market. If a few peasants became rich under the new system, so much the better; their success would serve as an example to others.

By Western standards, economic freedom was still heavily restricted, but the Chinese people grabbed the new opportunities. In the countryside, the responsibility system stimulated a rapid rise in agricultural production. Free markets sprang up in villages and cities to sell the increase. Entrepreneurs—often young people waiting for government job assignments after finishing school—set up restaurants, photography studios, repair shops, and a host of other small businesses in the cities. While keeping many of their old functions in housing, education, and medical care, communes—renamed "municipalities"—became freer places as people began making more decisions on their own.

ATTRACTING FOREIGN INVESTMENT

In 1979, Deng Xiaoping's government began creating "special economic zones" to attract foreign investment. The PRC would build factories, provide a cheap labor force, and grant low tax rates in exchange for large-scale investment and access to modern manufacturing methods. The industrial nations responded cautiously at first, but soon several zones were prospering.

Deng worked hard to improve ties with the outside world. The PRC and the United States established full diplomatic relations in January 1979. After decades of hostility, the PRC and the USSR began discussions to resolve border disputes. Overcoming bitter memories of World War II, China joined Japan in multibillion-dollar joint ventures to develop industries in the PRC. Britain and the PRC signed a treaty that would preserve Hong Kong's free enterprise system after the expiration of Britain's 99-year lease in 1997. The reunification of mainland China and Taiwan remained a thorny issue, but in the new atmosphere of openness, the Communist and Nationalist governments began exchanging ideas through scholars and business travelers. For the first time since the Communist revolution in 1949, overseas Chinese were allowed to visit families in the PRC.

THE DEMOCRACY WALL MOVEMENT

In the midst of the Four Modernizations, Deng and his pragmatic colleagues had little patience with Chinese students and intellectuals who warned that true modernization could not be achieved until the people were allowed to debate public policies and to decide for themselves China's future direction.

In November and December 1978, students plastered a wall near Beijing's Forbidden City with posters, poems, and essays calling for democratic reform. Wei Jingsheng, a young park attendant, became a leading speaker for the movement after he posted an essay arguing that democracy was "the fifth modernization," without which all the rest were meaningless. The Democracy Wall movement triggered demonstrations for civil rights in Beijing, Canton, Shanghai, and other cities. An edgy government struck back in January 1979 with mass arrests. Wei Jingsheng was sentenced to fifteen years in prison for illegal activities.

ECONOMIC TROUBLES

The government's sweeping economic reforms produced new problems for the PRC. In the countryside, grain production suffered as peasants turned to more profitable crops. Expensive equipment purchased by the communes for large-scale farming stood unused and rusting. Pollution and the expansion of rural manufacturing and housing destroyed precious farmland. Young people who had been forced by earlier government decrees to move to the countryside protested travel restrictions that prevented their return to the city. Rural poor people—and there were millions despite the new prosperity in the countryside—began drifting into already overcrowded cities in search of economic opportunity.

In the cities there was a shortage of decent jobs. Factory workers protested working conditions, scarce housing, and wages that lagged behind what many peasants were making under the responsibility system. Students, always the quickest to criticize government policies, demonstrated against conditions in the schools, inadequate financial aid, and programs that prepared them for careers where no jobs were available.

Corruption spread through the government as

Under the watchful eye of a British official, a Chinese work crew unpacks chests of opium. Trade in the illegal narcotic devastated Chinese society.

A Taiping charge breaks under the disciplined fire of the "Ever-Victorious Army," a Chinese force trained and led by Western officers.

Empress Dowager Cixi, the shrewd but tradition-bound ruler of China for fifty-seven years.

In 1898, the young emperor Guangxu made a bold attempt to initiate reform, but a furious Cixi imprisoned him, executed his advisers, and repealed his decrees.

Left: **T**he child Puyi, last emperor of China, gave up his throne in 1912.

Below: **D**r. Sun Yat-sen, first president of the Republic of China, and, behind him, his successor as leader of the Nationalists, Chiang Kai-shek.

Mao Zedong, the young radical who would eventually lead the Communists to victory against the Nationalists.

At the Whampoa military academy, foreign advisers trained a tough corps of young officers to lead the Nationalist armies in the fight against the warlords.

Mao Zedong on the Long March. With the warlords on the run, Chiang Kai-shek turned against his allies, the Communists. In 1934, the Communist Red Army began its epic 6,000-mile (9,600-km) retreat into China's desolate west.

A Japanese propaganda poster portrayed the invaders as friends of the Chinese peasants. The caption reads: "Put your trust in the Japanese military. Come back to your homes."

Communist guerrilla fighters fought the Japanese and, with increasing frequency, the armies of their nominal allies, the Nationalists.

In the fall of 1949, hundreds of thousands celebrated the Communist victory over the Nationalists and the formation of the People's Republic of China (PRC).

Peasants plow a commune field. Mao's disastrous series of agricultural reforms deprived the peasants of their land and destroyed much of their will to work.

Red Guards on the march in Shanghai in 1967. Thwarted by cautious planners in the government and the party, Mao sent millions of fanatical young people into the streets to wage the Great Proletarian Cultural Revolution.

In 1972, Chairman Mao Zedong and Premier Zhou Enlai met with President Richard Nixon and National Security Adviser Dr. Henry Kissinger in negotiations to reestablish ties between China and the United States.

Chairman Mao Zedong, China's "Great Helmsman," lies in state in September 1976.

A poster on Beijing's Democracy Wall denounces Mao's widow, the radical Jiang Qing, following the fall of the "Gang of Four" in 1976.

China's aging leadership in
June 1983: (left to right) Hu Yaobang,
Deng Xiaoping, Li Xiannian, Zhao Ziyang,
Deng Yingchao, and Peng Zhen.

Shoppers gather around a television display
in Chongging in 1992. Under Deng Xiaoping,
the government liberalized the economy and
made some luxuries available to China's
newly prosperous workers and peasants.

Above: In May 1989, pro-democracy students demand reforms similar to the *glasnost* policy of political openness promoted by Soviet General Secretary Mikhail Gorbachev.

Right: With demonstrations for democracy sweeping China, ebullient students crowd into trucks to carry their message through the streets.

Above: On May 17, 1989, more than a million Chinese gathered in Tiananmen Square to demonstrate for democracy. The Monument to the People's Martyrs and Mao's Tomb are in the background.

Right: Beijing University art students erect the "Goddess of Democracy" as a rallying point for the pro-democracy demonstrations in Tiananmen Square.

Right: In the early morning of June 4, 1989, pro-democracy crowds blocked troop convoys headed for Tiananmen Square. A photographer recorded the worker in the center pleading with the soldiers: "You cannot go and hurt your brothers and sisters."

Below: The night of June 4, 1989: as crowds battle army columns in the streets of Beijing, students committed to non-violence rescue a severely beaten soldier.

Daylight, June 5, 1989: a badly injured
demonstrator is rushed to the hospital.

A bid for the Olympics quickens our march towards 2000

申办奥运会奔向2000年

The People's Republic of China made a major bid to bring the Olympic Games for the year 2000 to Beijing. However, criticism of the government's human-rights record influenced the International Olympic Committee, and on September 23, 1993, the games were awarded to Sydney, Australia.

party cadres took bribes, put relatives in well-paid positions, and funneled consumer goods into an expanding black market. Foreign companies criticized the quality of Chinese labor in the new economic zones and refused to buy Chinese goods that did not meet their standards. The result was a serious trade imbalance that drained hard currency from the PRC and eventually left the government short of funds for public works.

In addition to these economic difficulties, the government faced numerous ongoing problems. Despite a vigorous program to control the birthrate, the population was expanding. Close to a quarter of the people were practically illiterate, and hundreds of millions more had only the barest education. Hostility with Vietnam led to repeated border clashes. Unrest in Tibet led to riots and brutal crackdowns by the Chinese authorities.

The bloodshed in Tibet was a reminder of the ruthless character of the Chinese leadership. Confronted with severe economic problems, Deng Xiaoping and the pragmatists were capable of daring reforms, but they would crush any challenge to the dominant position of the Communist party in Chinese society.

9 The Democracy Movement

As Deng Xiaoping's economic reforms ran into difficulty, students and intellectuals renewed their call for civil rights and a voice for the people in the decisions facing China. Democracy was such an alien concept that many students had only a vague idea of how it worked. Yet they believed that there was something wrong in a society where the government had so much power and the people so little.

Many civil rights commonplace in the West were unknown in China. Deng's government relaxed some controls to promote individual economic initiative. However, government officials still decided where people lived, what they could read, when and where they could travel, how long they continued in school, what employment opportunities they received, when they could marry, how many children they could have, and on down a long list of decisions that people in the West ordinarily made for themselves. Anyone who spoke out against the CCP or communism itself did so at great personal risk. Punishments ranged from public criticism by a cadre, to loss of job and privileges, to "reeducation" in a labor camp, to imprisonment, and finally—for the worst offenders—to public execution. Yet intellectuals and students persisted in their criticism of the system.

THE OBLIGATION OF AN EDUCATION

Since the time of the first scholar-mandarins more than 2,000 years before, people who sought a higher education in China had accepted special patriotic and moral obligations. In exchange for the great respect granted them by society, they were obligated to use their knowledge in the service of the country. When China strayed from the path of harmony, it was their moral obligation—freely sought and willingly accepted—to speak out, whatever the risks to livelihood, family, personal freedom, or life itself.

Time and again, Chinese intellectuals paid a terrible price. In old China, outspoken scholars were banished, tortured, and hanged on the order of emperors. As the dynastic system rotted, intellectuals formed underground societies to search for ways to save China. But time and again, imperial secret police smashed their organizations.

In 1898, the intellectuals nearly succeeded in reforming the old system when they engineered the Hundred Days Reform, but the empress dowager Cixi crushed the movement and imprisoned the liberal young emperor Guangxu. In the early twentieth century, scholars and students helped overthrow the last dynasty and spearheaded attempts to establish a republic, only to be disappointed as warlords and foreign interests destroyed it. Yet they did not give up. On May 4, 1919, students in Beijing launched the May Fourth Movement that energized China and led to changes that rocked the nation over the next half century.

Some of China's brightest young intellectuals took up the Communist banner. Brilliant, dedicated, and ruthless, they established communism in the world's most populous nation and built a radically new system. But by the late 1980s, history was proving that communism was a flawed system that could not compete— or perhaps even survive—in a rapidly changing world. Grown old and inflexible, the revolutionary generation could not face that reality.

RUMBLINGS

The increasing efficiency of the electronic media made it difficult for the Chinese leadership to keep the people isolated. Radio and television broadcasts from Hong Kong, Taiwan, and Japan brought a steady flow of information and images revealing the widening gap between living standards in China and in the industrialized nations. Contact with overseas Chinese and Western visitors brought additional evidence that China, despite the Four Modernizations, was falling farther behind. The desire for material well-being was only part of the discontent of the Chinese people. More important was the universal hunger for human dignity and liberty—a hunger that would bring millions of Chinese into the streets to challenge the Communist system.

In December 1986, seven years after the crushing of the Democracy Wall movement, renewed protests for democracy, better living standards, and an end to official corruption broke out in Beijing, Shanghai, and a half dozen other cities. The government moved quickly to crush the protests, disciplining outspoken intellectuals and arresting the movement's ringleaders, who were accused of spreading the "spiritual pollution" of decadent capitalism. Among those dismissed from their jobs and the CCP were the scientist Fang Lizhi and the writer Liu Binyan. Hu Yaobang (1915–1989), the pro-reform secretary-general of the CCP, was made a scapegoat for the unrest and dismissed from office.

The imposed silence did not last. Late in 1988, as the PRC prepared to celebrate its fortieth anniversary, prominent writers and scientists wrote letters to Deng Xiaoping. They suggested that he use the anniversary for a radical overhaul of the CCP and the opening of the government to participation by China's masses. Deng, beset with problems in the economy, harshly dismissed the intellectuals' pleas.

On April 15, 1989, the popular Hu Yaobang died. Student leaders organized memorial demonstrations for better schools, an end to corruption, the release of political prisoners, and the beginning of democratic reform. They spread their call for action through wall posters, leaflets, and even fax machines and computer networks. Word of mouth did the rest.

TIANANMEN SQUARE

The demonstrations that the world would identify with Beijing's great public square began on April 17, 1989. That morning, thousands of students poured into Tiananmen Square to put flowers and posters beneath a large portrait of Hu placed on the Monument to the People's Martyrs. Throughout the day, student groups marched to the monument, where they listened to speeches, sang revolutionary songs, and chanted slogans calling for reform within the Communist system.

The next day a larger crowd assembled. A student leader climbed the monument to read a list of demands through a bullhorn. The crowd cheered the call for freedom of speech and assembly, a larger education budget, a reevaluation of Hu Yaobang's contribution to the PRC, and a new openness by China's leaders. It seemed mild stuff by Western standards, but the demands and the crowd's reaction represented a direct challenge to the Chinese leadership. In an act of unprecedented bravado, several hundred students began a sit-in near the entrance of the Great Hall of the People. Several thousand more demonstrated in front of the Zhong-nanhai, the walled compound west of the square where many Communist leaders lived.

At dawn on April 19, some 500 police pushed the demonstrators away from the main gate of the Zhong-nanhai. But after a day of protests in the square, twice the number of students returned to the compound to demand an audience with Premier Li Peng (1928–). Police charged, beating and kicking protesters before arresting perhaps 150 of the fleeing crowd. The next day it rained hard, reducing the crowds to a stubborn few hundred and turning Beijing a gloomy gray. The city government announced that demonstrators would be "dealt with severely."

MASS PROTEST

The students ignored the warning. When sunshine returned on April 21, 100,000 demonstrators poured into Tiananmen Square in a protest that soon dwarfed any spontaneous demonstration in the history of the PRC. In some 200 cities across China, people gathered by the tens of thousands to show their support for the Beijing demonstrations. The students hoped to win the attention of Zhao Ziyang (1919–), Hu Yaobang's successor as secretary-general of the CCP and a leader considered more flexible than Deng Xiaoping or the hard-line Li Peng. But Zhao did not appear. The next day, as officials gathered for Hu's memorial services in the Great Hall of the People, an estimated 200,000 people gathered in the square to demand a dialogue with the leadership.

The leadership remained silent, hoping that the demonstrations would fade after Hu's memorial services. Instead, the student leaders increased the pressure. On April 24, as daily protests continued in the square, students at Beijing University began a boycott of classes that quickly spread to universities across China. The students formed independent unions in a direct challenge to the law forbidding the formation of any organization not approved by the CCP.

On April 26, the *People's Daily*, the CCP's official newspaper, labeled the democracy movement "a planned conspiracy [intended to] throw society into chaos and destroy the peaceful united political system." Meant to frighten the students, the editorial only deepened their resolve to do their patriotic duty by protesting the unfairness and corruption of the system. The next day saw the biggest demonstration yet, as 250,000 people marched into central Beijing. Thousands of workers left their factories to help the students force their way through the police barricades surrounding Tiananmen Square. Delegations of army officers, news reporters, and government officials joined the march to show support for changes in the system.

THE GOVERNMENT SOFTENS

Confronting a protest movement that was growing rather than fading, the government showed signs of flexibility. Over the next several days, student and government leaders met to talk. But the government refused to recognize the independent student unions, and the students refused to negotiate until it did. The students again called for mass protests. On May 4, the seventieth anniversary of China's most famous protest movement, 100,000 chanting, sign-waving students marched down the broad streets leading to the square. In a gesture, part irony, part plea, one group sang the words of the Chinese national anthem as they passed the Zhongnanhai compound: "Rise ye who refuse to be slaves."

For a week after the May 4 march, both the government and the students backed away from open confrontation. Zhao Ziyang delivered a speech to foreign bank officials that seemed to promise that the government would address the protesters' concerns. Most of the students returned to classes. But the quiet was deceptive as the capital prepared for a long-anticipated event.

THE GORBACHEV VISIT

Deng Xiaoping had carefully orchestrated a warming of relations with the USSR after nearly thirty years of hostility. To signify the new friendship between the Communist giants, Deng had invited Soviet General Secretary Mikhail Gorbachev (1931–) to visit Beijing in the middle of May. The long-planned Gorbachev visit had become a major worry for Deng and the senior Chinese leadership. Renewed student demonstrations would cause the leadership to lose face in the eyes of the world, but to crack down on the students might force Gorbachev to cancel his trip, putting years of diplomacy at risk.

The students awaited Gorbachev's visit with enthusiasm. The smiling, progressive Gorbachev was stunningly unlike the grim Soviet leaders of the past. He had relaxed Soviet control over Eastern Europe and opened a dialogue with the United States that promised a new era of cooperation between the superpowers. At home, he had initiated a policy of open political discussion, called *glasnost*, while pursuing a more cautious program of economic reform, called *perestroika*. Gorbachev's program of reviving the Soviet economy by inviting wider public participation in the government stood in stark contrast to Deng's strategy of instituting radical economic reforms while keeping a tight lid on personal liberties and political expression.

HUNGER STRIKE

While the Chinese government appealed to the students to refrain from demonstrations during Gorbachev's visit, student leaders began planning protests calling for Chinese *glasnost*. On May 13, tens of thousands of students again gathered in Tiananmen Square. Some 3,000 put on white headbands and began a hunger strike for democratic reform. Supporters set up camp around the strikers. By the time Gorbachev flew into Beijing two days later, thousands of students were sleeping in the square. During the day, the crowds swelled to well over 100,000. Student leaders—once concerned only with getting people to demonstrate—were now confronted with the task of providing food, water, and sanitation for crowds beyond anyone's expectations. The government—its orders ignored and its police outnumbered many times over—shifted welcoming ceremonies for Gorbachev from the Great Hall of the People to the airport.

On May 16, the crowd in the square numbered several hundred thousand. Greatly embarrassed by the protests, Chinese officials whisked Gorbachev through a back door into the Great Hall of the People for a meeting with Deng Xiaoping and other senior leaders. Outside in the square, the festive mood of the crowd was dampened as dozens of hunger strikers collapsed and were rushed by ambulance to hospitals.

The hunger strike was a novel tactic in the long history of Chinese protest, and it touched a sensitive cultural nerve. For thousands of years, the vast majority of Chinese had farmed the land, persevering through drought, flood, pestilence, war, and famine. For the Chinese, the raising of crops was more than an occupation; it was a sacred undertaking. They enjoyed the good times, but always with a cautious thrift in case hard times came again. Probably in no other nation on earth had concern for the next meal played a more consistent part in daily life. That anyone would risk death by starvation to make a political protest was nearly unthinkable. But several thousand students were doing just that in Tiananmen Square.

By the evening of May 16, some 350 hunger strikers had been hospitalized. Vowing to bear witness to the strikers' sacrifice, tens of thousands of people camped in the square that night. For the first time in the history of the PRC, Chinese newspapers and television stations ignored government censorship to report on the demonstrations and the plight of the hunger strikers. Shortly after midnight, Zhao Ziyang sent a message from the Politburo Standing Committee promising "concrete measures to enhance democracy and law, oppose corruption, build an honest and clean government, and expand openness." In return, he begged the protesters to return to their schools and jobs. A day or two before, Zhao's message might have won that restraint, but it was too late. The dam had burst and leaders on both sides could only fight to stay afloat in the titanic wave of protest sweeping the nation.

THE ASTONISHING SEVENTEENTH

At dawn on the morning of May 17, 1989, more than a million Chinese marched toward Tiananmen Square. The students were a minority among the factory workers, peasants, government employees, intellectuals, journalists, and even soldiers and police in the flood of demonstrators. Thousands of banners—many with inscriptions of newly formed independent student, craft, and labor unions—waved above the crowd. The Chinese leaders were again forced to direct Gorbachev's motorcade to a rear entrance of the Great Hall of the People. But nothing could conceal the immense outpouring of hope that had filled Tiananmen Square with a sea of humanity. Foreign television crews circulated through the crowd, beaming the scene to an astonished world.

On May 18, as a bemused Gorbachev left China, a million people again gathered in the square. In the aftermath of what should have been a public relations triumph, the Chinese leadership faced a desperate choice: world condemnation if they called in the army to crush the democracy movement; or the possible destruction of the Communist system if they gave in to the protesters. Premier Li Peng met with student leaders, but neither side would yield an inch.

In the predawn of May 19, Zhao Ziyang visited the hunger strikers, tearfully apologizing for coming so late and again promising to push for reform. He begged them to end their fast, but most refused. By day's end, some 2,400 of the 3,000 strikers were hospitalized. Zhao tried to find support for compromise within the Communist leadership. But Deng Xiaoping backed Li Peng and the other hard-liners in their determination to take strong action. On the night of May 19, Li Peng and President Yang Shangkun declared martial law.

On May 20, troop convoys rumbled into the outskirts of Beijing. In street after street, crowds chanting "patriotism is no crime" blocked the troops. Most of the young soldiers knew little of the democracy movement and had expected to find "hooligans" disrupting the city. Instead, they saw Chinese of every age and every walk of life peaceably protesting. As their loyalties began to waver, officers hastily pulled back the convoys.

STANDOFF

Giving in to pleas from other protesters, the hunger strikers gave up their fast on May 20. Three days later, a million demonstrators marched through the streets of Beijing, demanding Li Peng's resignation and the retirement of Deng Xiaoping.

The students' round-the-clock occupation of Tiananmen Square entered its second week. To pass the time, the students played music, danced, and debated the form a Chinese democracy should take. The strain of days of poor food, unsanitary conditions, and little sleep showed in their faces. Hundreds drifted back to their universities. Exhausted student leaders began discussing an end to the mass demonstrations and the adoption of lower-key protests. But thousands of fresh students were arriving from universities all over China, and they would not hear of abandoning the square. Some Beijing art students erected a 33-foot (10-m) plaster and Styrofoam figure of a young woman holding a raised torch, somewhat reminiscent of the Statue of Liberty in New York harbor. "The Goddess of Democracy" became the rallying point for the students holding doggedly to the square.

PRELUDE TO TRAGEDY

Paralyzed a week before, the government was now firmly in the hands of the hard-liners. Zhao Ziyang had disappeared from sight and was rumored to be under house arrest. Some 200,000 troops surrounded Beijing. Military leaders, at first hesitant to use force against the demonstrators, signaled their willingness to follow orders.

The increased participation of workers in the demonstrations had tipped the scales in favor of the hard-liners. Students might put down their books for a few weeks and shout themselves hoarse without doing real damage. But workers organized into independent trade unions represented a deadly threat to the government's control of the economy and quite possibly to the CCP itself. With the crowds in Tiananmen Square thinning but the independence of the workers increasing, the government decided to use force.

Shortly after midnight on June 3, army truck convoys entered the Beijing suburbs. They were halted at barricades and quickly surrounded by angry citizens who lectured the soldiers on the democracy movement. Some detachments withdrew; others sat stalled as night turned to day. It is not clear what the government intended with this weak and poorly coordinated effort. Perhaps the leadership thought that the lightly armed troops could occupy central Beijing without spilling blood. A more sinister theory suggested that the leaders wanted to bait the workers into a confrontation that the government could use as an excuse for an all-out attack.

As news of the troop movements swept across Beijing, crowds streamed into the streets of the working-class neighborhoods surrounding the square. Pledging to defend the students, the crowds blocked intersections with lines of buses and concrete traffic barriers. Occasional scuffles broke out, as the spring sun beat down on the crowds and on the confused, often frightened soldiers in the stalled convoys. Student leaders hurried to intervene between soldiers and workers, insisting that the demonstrators hold to the principle of nonviolence. But about 2:00 P.M., soldiers and riot police stormed out of the Zhongnanhai compound, firing tear gas and swinging riot sticks. Instead of fleeing, the crowd fought back with rocks and clubs. The attackers retreated.

In Tiananmen Square, about 20,000 students kept their vigil. Some hoped that the people of Beijing could hold back the army indefinitely, but most accepted the inevitable confrontation. They prepared masks for the expected clouds of tear gas and readied themselves for clubs and rubber bullets. Few students expected the soldiers to use deadly force.

MASSACRE

As night fell, the army's convoys still sat stalled a mile or more from the square. Crowds had blocked the largest column with a barricade of buses about three and a half miles from the southwest entrance to Tiananmen Square. About 10:30 P.M., twenty armored personnel carriers charged the barricade. They smashed through, crushing demonstrators under their tracks. Firing machine guns, the personnel carriers roared into the working-class neighborhoods along the Changan Boulevard. The crowds fought back with rocks, firebombs, and clubs, slowing the column at every intersection.

The course of the fighting over the next four hours is almost impossible to trace. Several army columns converged on the square, all at least temporarily halted by barricades and worker resistance. Some troops abandoned their vehicles rather than fire on the people, and crowds set fire to dozens of empty trucks and personnel carriers. A number of soldiers who used their weapons on the people were waylaid and beaten to death, but many more soldiers were saved by students and workers who risked their own safety to rescue them from maddened crowds.

Most of the bloodshed occurred along Changan Boulevard as the main assault force plowed through barricades and crowds, leaving thousands of civilians dead or wounded. The fighting was particularly heavy at the Xidan intersection, about a mile from the square. But unarmed civilians were no match for machine guns and armored vehicles. Soon hospitals and morgues overflowed with casualties from the massacre along "bloody boulevard."

THE RETAKING OF TIANANMEN

A few thousand resolute students waited in Tiananmen Square. The dull light of burning buses and army vehicles glowed beyond the Great Hall of the People as tracer bullets arced over Mao's tomb. Some students left to fight; those committed to nonviolence gathered near the Goddess of Liberty. They linked hands and sang.

About 2:00 A.M. on June 4, the army broke through

to the square. Eyewitness accounts of the next three hours vary widely. Apparently the troops took positions around the square to await further orders. Police officers isolated foreign journalists, arresting a few and demanding film and videotapes from the others. A crowd of students marched toward the soldiers to show their defiance. With or without orders, some soldiers fired, killing at least a few students and perhaps many more.

At 4:00 A.M., the lights around the square went out. Fearing an all-out attack, the rock star Hou Dejian desperately begged officers for time to let the students leave in peace. At 4:30 A.M., the lights went back on, and a government loudspeaker announced that the students could leave. Singing "The *Internationale*," the old anthem of world revolution, the students marched down a corridor of heavily armed soldiers and out of the square. But there they ran into an army column which, apparently, had not been informed that the students had permission to leave. The lead tank charged, crushing perhaps ten students and sending the others fleeing. Soldiers opened fire, cutting down many more.

Inside the square, an armored personnel carrier toppled the Goddess of Democracy. Other personnel carriers methodically destroyed the students' camp. Student leaders later claimed that dozens—perhaps hundreds—of students waiting to surrender were crushed as the personnel carriers ran over the tents. Bulldozers pushed the debris—and, according to some reports, scores of bodies—into a huge bonfire at the center of the square. A column of oily smoke rose into the Beijing morning.

AFTERMATH

It took the army several days to stamp out resistance in Beijing and some eighty other cities across China. The government began widespread arrests. The outspoken scientist Fang Lizhi and his wife sought protection inside the United States embassy. Other protest leaders escaped abroad, but most were imprisoned. Thousands of students were hustled off to "reeducation" camps.

The government imposed a ban on independent news reporting. Only fragmentary—and often wildly inaccurate—stories reached the outside world. Since most reporters and television crews had seen only the chaos in Tiananmen Square, few stories reported the heavy fighting along Changan Boulevard. Also lost was an understanding in the minds of most readers and viewers of the CCP's motivation for using force, not so much to crush the fading student protests as to smash the emerging power of the independent labor unions. In the end, the remaining students in Tiananmen Square became the bait the government needed to bring the workers into the streets, where the tanks and armored personnel carriers took their terrible toll.

Spokesmen for the Chinese government downplayed the violence, blaming the "incident" on a few "hooligans and counterrevolutionary elements." At one point, government officials blamed the entire affair on the staff of a Beijing radio station that they charged was controlled by the American Central Intelligence Agency. Understandably, student leaders who survived the crackdown tried to paint the government in the worst possible hues. Their stories of hundreds of students gunned down or crushed and then burned in Tiananmen Square were probably exaggerated. But neither denial nor exaggeration could disguise the fact that there was great violence in Beijing on the night of June 3–4, 1989.

How many were killed or injured may never be known. Estimates range from 300 to 3,000 killed and from 6,000 to 30,000 injured. Military and civilian police arrested at least 30,000 people and perhaps tens of thousands more. Courts were particularly savage in dealing with workers. Of the 60 or more protest leaders executed, most were workers.

Across China, millions of people were subjected to "reeducation" in their schools and communities. The People's Liberation Army was portrayed as the savior of the revolution and the great defender of the people. Schoolchildren were taught songs that praised the PLA and that pledged their own eternal vigilance against enemies of the revolution. Young and old alike spoke with seeming sincerity about the wisdom of Deng Xiaoping, Mao Zedong, and the other leaders of the revolutionary generation. After years of declining power, party cadres again watched for the least deviation from the "party line." Parroting the CCP's propaganda when they had to, whispering of a better tomorrow when they could, the Chinese people—their brief spring of exuberant freedom extinguished—settled in to wait for the next turn in the long cycle of Chinese history.

10 Since Tiananmen

The horrifying pictures of fire and carnage in Tiananmen Square outraged people around the world. The world's democracies condemned the actions of China's leaders. But the outcry diminished quickly as governments became concerned that denunciations might do more harm than good.

The world's democracies faced a dilemma in choosing the best way to promote democratic change in China. Since the early 1970s, China had become an increasingly important diplomatic and military power. By inviting foreign investment and trade, China's leaders had taken a step toward improving the living standards of hundreds of millions of Chinese. Yet China's ties with the outside world were fragile. Many foreign leaders in government, business, and intellectual circles argued that trade, investment, and quiet diplomacy would benefit the Chinese people more than trade sanctions and heated criticism of China's leadership. In a world struggling to find peace and stability, no one wanted to see China's leaders again choosing isolation and hostility.

President George Bush (1924–), a former United States ambassador to China, directed a carefully non-confrontational policy in dealing with the PRC. Only weeks after the massacre, National Security Adviser Brent Scowcroft flew to Beijing to assure the Chinese leadership of America's continued interest in building diplomatic and economic ties. Bush vetoed a congressional bill granting permanent resident status to pro-democracy Chinese students studying in the United States, but he did extend the students' visas by executive order. At the request of the Bush administration, the PRC gave permission for Fang Lizhi to leave the United States embassy and China.

The Bush administration's policies were heatedly criticized in Congress, but the president refused to give in to demands for trade and diplomatic sanctions against the PRC. The cautious approach of the administration was a great disappointment to those who believed that strong and steady pressure was needed to promote democracy in China. Banding together, they lobbied Congress, organized seminars, and marked the first anniversaries of Tiananmen Square with fresh calls for stern measures against the government of the PRC.

COLLAPSE OF THE SOVIET EMPIRE

The world's attention was soon drawn away from China. In the amazing fourteen months following Tiananmen Square, the Soviet Empire in Eastern Europe collapsed. Allowed to choose their own future by Soviet leader Gorbachev, Poland, Czechoslovakia, Hungary, East Germany, Romania, and Bulgaria threw out their Communist regimes in favor of democratic governments. By the late summer of 1990, only fragmenting Yugoslavia and tiny Albania still had Communist governments.

The massive rejection of the Communist system spread to the Soviet Union itself. Gorbachev desperately tried to hold the USSR together, but by the second anniversary of Tiananmen Square, most Soviet republics were demanding self-government. In August 1991, Soviet hard-liners put Gorbachev under house arrest and took over the government. The Soviet people stormed into the streets by the hundreds of thousands to resist the coup. Refusing to fire on their fellow citizens, Soviet troops joined the demonstrators. Boris Yeltsin, president of the Russian Republic, mounted a tank to demand the ouster of the hard-liners. Within days, the coup leaders surrendered, and the people celebrated the triumph of democracy in Russia.

Over the next few months, the Soviet Union broke apart as its member states reasserted sovereignty over their affairs. Gorbachev was shunted to the sidelines and eventually resigned, as Yeltsin and the leaders of the other republics discussed an alliance that has yet to assume a firm outline. The collapse of the Soviet Union left the PRC as the only remaining Communist power. As even the hard-line regimes in Albania and the Mongolian People's Republic moved toward democracy, only Cuba and the PRC still held to the Communist line.

THE QUIET REVOLUTION

Communism is in deep trouble in China. The majority of the people have lost faith in the system and in the CCP's aged leaders. In an effort to revive patriotic memories of the revolution, the CCP recently brought back the cult of Mao Zedong. His picture is seen everywhere, souvenir shops again stock Mao memorabilia, and the story of his revolutionary years is told again and again in films and plays. But few people pay attention to the propaganda, and almost no one reads the thought of Mao Zedong. When asked to name a hero, most people choose Premier Zhou Enlai, the wise, pragmatic "elder brother" who worked so hard to better the lives of the Chinese people.

Although still compelled to mouth the party line,

most people do so without enthusiasm. Armed soldiers still guard university gates, but the students speak with candor about their ambitions to pursue useful lives free of the direction of the party. The CCP is aging quickly as fewer young people join. Soon the party may have difficulty fielding enough able cadres to enforce its policies.

Barred from a meaningful voice in the government, the people are pursuing economic opportunity with a vengeance that threatens to destroy communism from within. Private enterprises are earning substantial profits, while inefficient state enterprises run up huge debts. Foreign trade is rising as Chinese electronic and consumer products approach world standards in quality. Foreign companies—many owned by wealthy overseas Chinese—are investing huge sums in free enterprise zones in coastal China. Today, many party officials and senior army officers seem more interested in cutting business deals than in carrying out their duties as defenders of the Communist system.

Although millions of Chinese are enjoying higher living standards, the revolution in the economy has produced strains. Corruption, waste, pollution, inflation, unemployment, energy shortfalls, and an inadequate transportation network are problems that need urgent remedies. An emerging class of well-to-do peasants is transforming the economy of rural China, but poverty remains widespread among the 800 million people still living on the land. Millions of dwellings lack running water, electricity, and indoor plumbing, and tens of millions of poor people survive without adequate nutrition, health care, or educational opportunities. And, as always, population growth represents a staggering problem for the future of the world's most populous nation.

Two-thirds of China's population of 1.15 billion is under the age of thirty-five. The culture of the young has little patience with drab "Mao suits"; politically acceptable music, film, and art; or the endless trumpeting of the CCP's four principles—socialism, the dictatorship of the people, the leadership of the CCP, and Marxist-Leninist–Mao Zedong thought. In their quest for democracy, justice, and opportunity lies the hope of China.

CYCLE UPON CYCLE

The cycle of birth, maturity, decay, dissolution, and rebirth occurs and reoccurs across three thousand years of Chinese history. Dynasty after dynasty came to power with forceful leaders and dynamic ideas. The dynasties accomplished great things in their maturity, but each fell into decline and was eventually swept away by internal revolt or foreign invasion. It often took years of turmoil before a new dynasty cemented its power, but through all the chaos, the Chinese people carried on with their lives. To be Chinese often meant suffering, but it was suffering with dignity, hope, and a firm belief in the eternal greatness of China.

When an ancient dynasty fell, the Chinese spoke of the changing mandate of heaven. In this century, the mandate of heaven has been replaced by the mandate of the people. The Chinese Communist Party has lost that mandate and will never regain it. Aged and increasingly out of touch with the people, the leaders of the revolutionary generation will disappear from the scene within a few years. Communism will probably survive at least a while longer under younger leaders. Whether these new leaders will be hard-liners or reformers will probably depend on which side the People's Liberation Army takes. Yet whichever side governs China at the close of the twentieth century, the restless Chinese people will continue to push the nation toward democracy. In the opening years of the new century, it seems increasingly likely that the Chinese people will at last succeed in taking the future into their own hands.

Source Notes

GENERAL SOURCES

In writing *China Past–China Future*, I depended heavily on a number of general source works. Each of the following contributed something to nearly every chapter: Caroline Blunden and Mark Elvin, *Cultural Atlas of China* (New York: Facts on File, 1983); Alasdair Clayre, *The Heart of the Dragon* (Boston: Houghton Mifflin, 1985); Robert F. Dernberger et al., eds., *The Chinese: Adapting the Past, Building the Future* (Ann Arbor: University of Michigan Center for Chinese Studies, 1986); *Encyclopaedia Britannica*, 15th ed. (1987); Keith Lye and Shirley Carpenter, eds., *Encyclopedia of World Geography* (New York: Dorset Press, 1989); John K. Fairbank, *China: A New History* (Cambridge, Mass.: Harvard University Press, 1992); C. P. Fitzgerald, *China: A Short Cultural History*, 3rd ed. (New York: Holt, Rinehart & Winston, 1961), and *The Horizon History of China* (New York: American Heritage, 1969); John S. Major *The Land and the People of China* (New York: J. B. Lippincott, 1989); National Geographic Society, *Journey into China* (Washington, D.C.: 1982); Lucian W. Pye, *China: An Introduction* (Boston: Little, Brown, 1972); Jonathan D. Spence, *The Search for Modern China* (New York: W. W. Norton, 1990); Geoffrey Barraclough, ed., *The Times Concise Atlas of World History* (Maplewood, N.J.: Hammond, 1985).

ADDITIONAL SOURCES

In addition to the above, I drew on the following periodicals and books for current information or for facts on specific periods in Chinese history:

Chapter 1, China: Most Populous Nation on Earth: *Beijing Review* (San Francisco: China Books); *China Briefing* (Boulder, Colo.: Westview Press, annual); *China Pictorial* (San Francisco: China Books); *China Today* (San Francisco: China Books); *Collier's Encyclopedia*, 1988 ed.; *Encyclopedia Americana* (1989 ed.); Stacey Peck, *Halls of Jade, Walls of Stone: Women in China Today* (New York: Franklin Watts, 1985); The Statesman's Year-book 1991–92, 128th ed. (New York: St. Martin's, 1991); *The World Almanac and Book of Facts* (New York: Pharos Books, 1992).

Chapters 2 and 3, The First Chinese; Emperors, Dynasties, and Mandarins: Editors of *Horizon* Magazine, *The Horizon Book of the Arts of China* (New York: American Heritage, 1969); Walter A. Fairservis, Jr., *The Origins of Oriental Civilization* (New York: New American Library, 1959); Edward H. Schafer, *Ancient China* (New York: Time-Life, 1967).

Chapter 4, Invaders from the North: Peter Brent, *Genghis Khan: The Rise, Authority and Decline of Mongol Power* (New York: McGraw-Hill, 1976); Leo de Hartog, *Genghis Khan: Conqueror of the World* (New York: St. Martin's, 1989).

Chapter 5, A Collision of Cultures: Burton F. Beers, *China in Old Photographs, 1860–1910* (New York: Dorset Press, 1981); Maxine Hong Kingston, *The Woman Warrior* (New York: Alfred A. Knopf, 1977); *The Travels of Marco Polo* (New York: Orion, 1958); Alfred Tamarin and Shirley Glubok, *Voyaging to Cathay: Americans in the China Trade* (New York: Viking, 1976); Chester Tan, *The Boxer Catastrophe* (New York: Columbia University Press, 1955).

Chapter 6, Decades of Turmoil: Harrison E. Salisbury, *China: 100 Years of Revolution* (New York: Holt, Rinehart & Winston, 1983); Edgar Snow, *Red Star Over China*, rev. ed. (New York, Grove Press, 1989); Jonathan D. Spence, *The Gate of Heavenly Peace: The Chinese and Their Revolution, 1895–1980* (New York: Viking, 1981); Barbara W. Tuchman, *Stilwell and the American Experience in China, 1911–45* (New York: Macmillan, 1970); Dick Wilson, *When Tigers Fight: The Story of the Sino-Japanese War, 1937–1945* (New York: Viking, 1982).

Chapter 7, The Building of the People's Republic: Asia Research Centre, *The Great Cultural Revolution in China* (Rutland, Vt.: Charles E. Tuttle, 1968); Gordon A. Bennet and Ronald N. Montaperto, *Red Guard: The Political Biography of Dai Hsiao-Ai* (New York: Doubleday, 1971); David Wen-Wei Chang, *Zhou Enlai and Deng Xiaoping in the Chinese Leadership Succession Crisis* (Lanham, Md.: University Press of America, 1984); Han Suyin, *Wind in the Tower: Mao Tsetung and the Chinese Revolution, 1949–1975* (Boston: Little, Brown, 1976); W. J. F. Jenner, ed., *China: A Photohistory 1937–1987* (New York: Pantheon, 1988); Liang Heng and Judith Shapiro, *Son of the Revolution* (New York: Alfred A. Knopf, 1983); *Quotations from Chairman Mao Tse-tung* (New York: Bantam, 1967).

Chapter 8, New Hopes, Broken Hopes: David Wen-Wei Chang, *China Under Deng Xiaoping: Political and Economic Reform* (New York: St. Martin's, 1988); Uli Franz, *Deng Xiaoping* (Orlando, Fla.: Harcourt Brace Jovanovich, 1988); John Frazer, *The Chinese: Portrait of a People* (New York: Summit Books, 1980); Ross Terrill, ed., *The China Difference* (New York: Harper & Row, 1979).

Chapters 9 and 10, The Democracy Movement; Since Tiananmen: Associated Press, *China from the Long March to Tiananmen Square* (New York: Henry Holt, 1990); Fang Lizhi, *Bringing Down the Great Wall: Writings on Science, Culture and Democracy in China* (New York: Alfred A. Knopf, 1991); Human Rights in China, *Children of the Dragon* (New York: Collier Books, 1990); Liu Binyan, *Tell the World: What Happened in China and Why* (New York: Pantheon, 1989), and *China's Crisis, China's Hope: Essays from an Intellectual in Exile* (Cambridge, Mass.: Harvard University Press, 1990); Andrew J. Nathan, *China's Crisis: Dilemmas of Reform and Prospects for Democracy* (New York: Columbia University Press, 1990); Scott Simmie and Bob Nixon, *Tiananmen Square* (Seattle: University of Washington Press, 1989).

China's democracy movement, the government's reaction to it, and the economic, political, and social dilemmas plaguing China's modernization have received extensive coverage in the print and broadcast media. In attempting to provide an analysis of these events and issues, I have found the coverage provided by *Newsweek, Time,* the *Wall Street Journal,* the *New York Times,* the *Christian Science Monitor,* the *Washington Post,* the *Nation,* the *New Republic,* CNN, and PBS of particular value. To their reporters, as well as to the authors of the books listed above, I would like to express my gratitude.

Suggested Reading

NONFICTION

Associated Press. *China from the Long March to Tiananmen Square.* New York: Henry Holt, 1990.

Beers, Burton F. *China in Old Photographs, 1860–1910.* New York: Dorset Press, 1981.

Blunden, Caroline, and Mark Elvin. *Cultural Atlas of China.* New York: Facts on File, 1983.

China Briefing. Boulder, Colo.: Westview Press, annual.

China: The Land and the People. New York: Gallery Books, 1988.

Clayre, Alasdair. *The Heart of the Dragon.* Boston: Houghton Mifflin, 1985.

Editors of *Horizon* Magazine. *The Horizon Book of the Arts of China.* New York: American Heritage, 1969.

Fitzgerald, C. P. *The Horizon History of China.* New York: American Heritage, 1969.

Human Rights in China. *Children of the Dragon.* New York: Collier Books, 1990.

Jenner, W. J. F., ed. *China: A Photohistory 1937–1987.* New York: Pantheon, 1988.

Kingston, Maxine Hong. *The Woman Warrior.* New York: Alfred A. Knopf, 1977.

Major, John S. *The Land and the People of China.* New York: J. B. Lippincott, 1989.

National Geographic Society. *Journey into China.* Washington, D.C., 1982.

Peck, Stacey. *Halls of Jade, Walls of Stone: Women in China Today.* New York: Franklin Watts, 1985.

Pye, Lucian W. *China: An Introduction.* Boston: Little, Brown, 1972.

Salisbury, Harrison E. *China: 100 Years of Revolution.* New York: Holt, Rinehart & Winston, 1983.

Schafer, Edward H. *Ancient China.* New York: Time-Life, 1967.

Sinclair, Kevin. *Over China.* Los Angeles: Knapp Press, 1988.

FICTION

Birch, Cyril, ed. *Anthology of Chinese Literature*. New York: Evergreen Books, 1965.

Buck, Pearl S. *The Good Earth*. New York: John Day, 1931.

Hersey, John. *A Single Pebble*. New York: Alfred A. Knopf, 1956.

Lao She. *Cat Country*. William A. Lyell, Jr., trans. Columbus: Ohio State University Press, 1970.

————. *Rickshaw*. Jean M. James, trans. Honolulu: University Press of Hawaii, 1979.

Lord, Bette Bao. *Spring Moon*. New York: Harper & Row, 1981.

Tan, Amy. *The Joy-Luck Club*. New York: Putnam, 1989.

PERIODICALS

Beijing Review. San Francisco: China Books.

China Pictorial. San Francisco: China Books.

China Today. San Francisco: China Books.

TELEVISION AND FILM

Good Earth, The. Sidney Franklin, director. United States: 1937.

Great Wall, A. Peter Wang, director. United States and China: 1986.

Heart of the Dragon, The. Public Broadcasting System. United States: 1985.

Ju Dou. Ahang Yi-mou, director. China and Japan: 1989.

Last Emperor, The. Bernard Bertolucci, director. United States, Great Britain, Italy, and China: 1987.

Sand Pebbles, The. Robert Wise, director. United States: 1966.

Index

About
Alden R. Carter

Alden R. Carter is a former naval officer and teacher. Since 1984 he has been a writer for children and young adults. His nonfiction books cover a wide range of topics, including electronics, super-computers, radio, Illinois, Shoshoni Indians, the Alamo, the Battle of Gettysburg, the Colonial Wars, the War of 1812, the Mexican War, the Civil War, and the Spanish-American War. He has also written five books on the American Revolution: *War for Independence: The American Revolution; Colonies in Revolt; Darkest Hours; At the Forge of Liberty;* and *Birth of the Republic.* His novels *Growing Season* (1984), *Wart, Son of Toad* (1985), *Sheila's Dying* (1987), and *Up Country* (1989) were named to the American Library Association's annual list, Best Books for Young Adults. His fifth novel, *RoboDad* (1990), was hon-ored as Best Children's Fiction Book of the Year by the Society of Midland Authors. A devoted traveler, Mr. Carter has visited nearly forty countries in Europe, Asia, and Africa. Mr. Carter lives with his wife, Carol, and their children, Brian Patrick and Siri Morgan, in Marshfield, Wisconsin.

About
David Wen-Wei Chang

Dr. David Wen-Wei Chang is Rosebush Professor of Political Sci-ence at the University of Wisconsin–Oshkosh. A contributor to nu-merous academic journals in Asia and the United States, he is the author of three books in the field of Chinese studies. His latest book, *China under Deng Xiaoping: Political and Economic Reform* (Macmillan of London and St. Martin's Press, New York, 1989), was translated into Chinese in 1991 and sold widely in the People's Republic of China. Named a Senior Fulbright Lecturer in the summer of 1992, Dr. Chang returned to China to teach at the People's University of China in Beijing and to do research for his next book.